CHECK YOUR ENGLISH VOCABULARY FOR

HUMAN RESOURCES
AND PERSONNEL MANAGEMENT

by

Rawdon Wyatt

B L O O M S B U R Y

www.bloomsbury.com/reference

First edition published 2005
Bloomsbury Publishing Plc
38 Soho Square, London W1D 3HB

British Library Cataloguing in Publication Data
A catalogue entry for this book is available from the British Library
ISBN 0 7475 6997 5

Text computer typeset by Bloomsbury Publishing
Printed in Italy by Legoprint

Introduction

Who is this book for?

This book has been written for anyone working, or planning to work, in human resources and personnel management, and who wants to develop their vocabulary for this line of work. The various exercises throughout the book focus on the key vocabulary that you would expect to understand and use on a day-to-day basis.

The book is also useful for anyone working in other business-related areas (secretarial, administrative, accountancy, sales, business law, business management, etc) who wants to broaden their knowledge of business vocabulary.

How should you use the book?

When you use this book, you should not go through the exercises mechanically. It is better to choose areas that you are unfamiliar with, or areas that you feel are of specific interest or importance to yourself.

The exercises are accompanied by a full answer key at the back of the book. This key also gives you lots of other information that might be useful to you, as well as providing other words (synonyms, opposites, alternative words, etc) that are not covered in the exercises themselves.

It is important to record new words and expressions that you learn. Try to develop your own personal vocabulary 'bank' in a notebook or file. Review the words and expressions on a regular basis so that they become an active part of your vocabulary.

You will find it very helpful to use a dictionary when you do the exercises in this book. A good dictionary will give a clear definition of words and expressions, show you how they are pronounced, and give sample sentences to show how they are used in context. Many of the words, expressions and examples in this book have been taken or adapted from the *Bloomsbury Dictionary of Human Resources and Personnel Management* (ISBN 0 7475 6623 2). You will also find the *Bloomsbury Easier English Dictionary for Students* (ISBN 0 7475 6624 0) a useful reference source.

Further recommended reading and reference:

If you would like to learn more about Human Resources, these books are very useful:

- *An Introduction to Human Resource Management*
  by John Stredwick (Elsevier: ISBN 0 7506 4580 6)

- *Essentials of HRM*
  by Shaun Tyson and Alfred York (Butterworth Heinemann: ISBN 0 7506 4715 9)

Contents

There are 18 words connected with human resources in the box below. Use them to complete the sentences. The first one has been done for you as an example.

assessment • budget • ceiling • experience • facilities • forecast   interview • mediation • mismanagement • motivation • objective • ~~peak~~   potential • predecessor • retirement • session • stipulation • supervision

1. He has reached the _____*peak*_____ of his career.

2. This morning's staff development _____ will be held in the conference room.

3. There are very good sports _____ on the company premises.

4. Older staff are planning what they will do in _____.

5. They made a complete _____ of each employee's contribution to the organisation.

6. The company failed because of the chairman's _____ of capital assets.

7. The applicant was pleasant and had the right qualifications, but unfortunately he did not have any relevant _____.

8. Our main recruitment _____ is to have well-qualified staff.

9. The dispute was ended through the _____ of union officials.

10. Employees showing leadership _____ will be chosen for management training.

11. He took over the job from his _____ last May.

12. She is very experienced and can be left to work without any _____

13. What _____ has the government put on wage increases this year?

14. The contract has a _____ that the new manager has to serve a three-month probationary period.

15. I am going for an _____ for a new job next week.

16. We need to draw up a _____ for salaries for the coming year.

17. We believe that the sales manager's _____ of higher turnover next year is a bit optimistic.

18. I think our sales staff lack _____. They don't seem very keen and haven't been working well recently.

Also see: *Nouns 2* on page 2
              Wordbuilding 2 + 3 on pages 10, 11 and 12

© Bloomsbury Publishing Plc. For reference see *Dictionary of Human Resources and Personnel Management* (ISBN 0 7475 6623 2)

Nouns 2

Starting in the top-left corner, separate the letters below into 15 different words. You will find the words by reading from left to right and from right to left, following the directions of the arrows. When you have done this, use the words to complete sentences 1 - 15 below. There is one word you will not need. The first one has been done as an example.

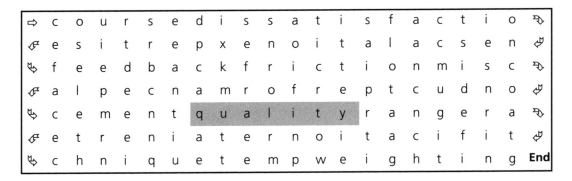

⇨	c	o	u	r	s	e	d	i	s	s	a	t	i	s	f	a	c	t	i	o	⇲
⇱	e	s	i	t	r	e	p	x	e	n	o	i	t	a	l	a	c	s	e	n	⇲
⇩	f	e	e	d	b	a	c	k	f	r	i	c	t	i	o	n	m	i	s	c	⇲
⇱	a	l	p	e	c	n	a	m	r	o	f	r	e	p	t	c	u	d	n	o	⇲
⇩	c	e	m	e	n	t	**q**	**u**	**a**	**l**	**i**	**t**	**y**	r	a	n	g	e	r	a	⇲
⇱	e	t	r	e	n	i	a	t	e	r	n	o	i	t	a	c	i	f	i	t	⇲
⇩	c	h	n	i	q	u	e	t	e	m	p	w	e	i	g	h	t	i	n	g	**End**

1. The poor ___quality___ of the service led to many complaints.

2. The agreement has to go to the board for _____.

3. We have had a _____ working in the office this week to clear the backlog of letters.

4. His overall _____ has improved considerably since he went on a management training course.

5. The salary _____ for this sort of job is between £17,000 and £19,000.

6. We hired Mr Smith because of his financial _____.

7. Although the work itself was interesting, there was a lot of _____ with the organisation and its rules.

8. When he disobeyed the orders he was given, he was dismissed for gross _____ .

9. There is a lot of _____ between the sales and accounts staff which we need to resolve as soon as possible.

10. The company sent her on a management _____ to help her develop her managerial skills.

11. She has finished university and is now looking for a _____ with a design agency.

12. Although he is a freelance worker, we don't want him to work for anyone else, so we pay him a _____ of £2,000.

13. London is an expensive city, so people working for our company there receive a £2,000 London _____ in addition to their salary.

14. The management received a lot of _____ on how popular the new pay scheme was proving.

15. The union has threatened an _____ in strike action.

Look at these dictionary definitions and the sample sentences which follow them, decide what words are being described and use them to complete the grid at the bottom of the page. To help you, some of the letters are already in the grid.

If you do this correctly, you will reveal a word in the shaded vertical strip which means 'to think again about a decision which has already been made'.

1. To search for and appoint new staff to join a company (*We need to _____ staff for our new store.*)

2. To give someone the power to do something (*Her new position will _____ her to hire and fire at will.*)

3. To ask an expert for advice (*Why don't you _____ your accountant about your tax?*)

4. To refuse to do something or to say that you do not accept something (*A lot of staff _____ to working on Saturdays.*)

5. To discuss a problem or issue formally with someone, so as to reach an agreement (*Before I accept the job, I'd like to _____ my contract.*)

6. To monitor work carefully to see that it is being done well (*I _____ six people in the accounts department.*)

7. To start a new custom or procedure (*We plan to _____ a new staff payment scheme.*)

8. To pass authority or responsibility to someone else (*He thinks he can do everything himself, and refuses to _____.*)

9. To calculate a value (*We need to _____ the experience and qualifications of all the candidates.*)

10. To examine something generally, usually before making changes (*We will _____ your salary after you have been with us for six months.*)

1.		E					T	
2.			P		W			
3.			S		L			
4.	O		J					
5.		E			T			
6.			P			V		
7.				T			T	
8.				E	G			
9.		V				A		
10.			V			W		

© Bloomsbury Publishing Plc. For reference see *Dictionary of Human Resources and Personnel Management* (ISBN 0 7475 6623 2)

Verbs 2

Rearrange the letters in **bold** in these sentences to make verbs (the dictionary definitions after each sentence will help you to decide what the verb is), and write the answers in the grid on the right. The *last* letter of one verb is the *first* letter of the next verb. The first one has been done for you as an example.

1. It usually takes about two weeks to **sorpsce** an insurance claim *(to deal with something in the usual routine way)*

2. The company has offered to **osonrsp** three employees for a management training course *(to pay for someone to go on a training course)*

3. She has been asked by her company to **hereracs** the effectiveness of bargaining structures *(to study a subject in detail)*

4. If our advertisement for a manager is unsuccessful, I suggest we **aedunhht** elsewhere *(to look for managers and offer them jobs in other companies)*

5. We would like to **ratsenrf** you to our Scottish branch *(to move someone or something to a new place)*

6. I would certainly **emredconm** Ms Smith for the job *(to say that someone or something is good)*

7. The manager had to **cenpisilid** three members of staff for their bad attitude at work *(to punish an employee for misconduct)*

8. The directors **peltoxi** their employees, who have to work hard for very little pay *(to use something to make a profit, usually used in a negative way)*

9. This company sells products that **gttrea** the teenage market *(to aim to sell to somebody)*

10. When his mistake was discovered, he offered to **nerted** his resignation *(to give / hand in: a formal word)*

11. If you accept the job, we can **wrerda** you with a generous remuneration package *(to give a person something in return for effort or achievement)*

12. Problems began when the workers decided to **gaisdrder** the instructions of the shop stewards *(to take no notice of, or not to obey)*

13. Mr Lee has been asked to **tirdce** our South-East Asian operations *(to manage or organise)*

14. I'm afraid we have no option but to **rmetintea** your contract with immediate effect *(to end something, or bring something to an end)*

15. The company is trying to **renugecoa** sales by giving large discounts *(to make it easier for something to happen)*

The grid on the right contains, in the top cell: *process*

Also see: *Changes* on pages 34 and 35

4

Look at these mini-dialogues. For each one, decide what has happened, is happening or will happen. Use the verbs from the box. In most cases, you will need to change the form of the verb.

appoint • accuse • assume • claim • collaborate • erode • fund • invite • justify
minimise • observe • qualify • question • validate • violate

1. Ms Jameson: Did you know that this company has a no smoking policy?
                   Put that cigarette out, please.
    Michael: Sorry, Ms Jameson. I won't do it again.

    Michael has just _____ one of the company rules.

2. Rick: We need to keep our labour costs as small as possible.
    Jan: In that case, we should only hire workers when we need them.

    The company wants to _____ its labour costs.

3. Mr Harrison: How's business with you at the moment?
    Ms Withers: It's very good. In fact, we're so busy, we've had to increase our
                   sales staff.

    Ms Withers' company has recently _____ some new staff.

4. Ms Jones: Could you check these sales figures to make sure they're correct?
    Mr Allen: Of course. I'll get back to you later with the results.

    Ms Jones wants Mr Allen to _____ the sales figures.

5. Richard: Mark, we have reason to believe that you've been selling confidential company
             information to another company.
    Mark: That's ridiculous. I would never do such a thing.

    Richard is _____ one of his colleagues of doing something illegal.

6. Mr Hendrik: I don't think the sales department should have got such a large bonus this year.
    Ms Newman: I disagree. They're worked extremely hard and achieved excellent results.

    Ms Newman is _____ the sales department's bonus.

7. Eric: I think it's great that our two companies are working together on this project.
    Mary: Me too. Between us, we've got some real expertise.

    Eric and Mary's companies are _____ with each other on a project.

8. Lisa: Did you break your arm at work?
    Laurence: Yes, and because it was the company's fault, I've asked for some money for
                 compensation.

    Laurence has just _____ damages from his company.

© Bloomsbury Publishing Plc. For reference see *Dictionary of Human Resources and Personnel Management* (ISBN 0 7475 6623 2)

9.   Mr White: Does the company have enough money to expand?
        Mr Roberts: No, but we're getting part of the money from the government.

The government is going to help _____ the company's expansion.

10.   Ms Colley: Your proposal is very interesting, but what would happen if
                       something went wrong?
        Ms Grant: Don't worry. Our company will accept responsibility for any
                       mistakes or errors.

Ms Grant's company will _____ all risks.

11.   Mr Rolfe: Have you had a chance to look at the latest sales figures?
        Ms Gomm: Yes, but are you sure they're accurate?

Ms Gomm is _____ the accuracy of the sales figures.

12.   Chris: Why is the staff canteen closed?
        Tim: The health and safety officer said that the canteen manager wasn't
                 obeying fire regulations.

The canteen manager failed to _____ fire regulations.

13   Ms Rooney: Why do secretaries in the sales department get paid more than
                       secretaries doing the same job in the HR department?
        Mr Beckham: I don't know, but over the next few months we will gradually
                       reduce the difference in salaries between the two departments.

Mr Beckham's company will _____ wage differentials between the two departments.

14.   Mr Langley: You've been here for six months, so you're entitled to some
                       paid leave.
        Ms Grey: That's great. I could do with a holiday.

Ms Grey has just _____ for paid leave.

15.   Jennifer: You look pleased with yourself? What's happened?
        Linda: I applied for a job last week, and I've been asked to go for an interview.

Linda has been _____ to attend an interview.

For more useful verbs, see *Changes* on page 34 and 35.

© Bloomsbury Publishing Plc. For reference see *Dictionary of Human Resources and Personnel Management* (ISBN 0 7475 6623 2)

Adjectives 1

In each of these sentences, you are given the first two letters of an adjective. Complete each adjective by using the other letters in the box. The first one has been done for you as an example.

-nstructive • -ccessful • -animous • -aggered • -laried • -oundless • -tional
-tonomous • -ntinuous • -nsultative • -ressful • -terprising • -lf confident
-ofessional • -filled • ~~-rmal~~ • -sciplinary • -ack

1.   Is this a fo_*rmal*_ job offer?

2.   There are still four un_____ places on the training course.

3.   The trainee was se_____ to the point of arrogance.

4.   We had to ask our lawyer for pr_____ advice on the contract.

5.   The union complained that the di_____ action was too harsh.

6.   Psychologists claim that repetitive work can be just as st_____ as more demanding but varied work.

7.   The complaint was proved to be gr_____.

8.   Attendance at staff meetings is op_____, although the management encourages employees to attend.

9.   The foreman decided to tighten up on sl_____ workers who were costing the company money.

10.   She made some co_____ suggestions for improving management-worker relations.

11.   The workforce in the factory is made up of several au_____ work groups.

12.   There was a un_____ vote against the proposal.

13.   The su_____ candidates for the job will be advised by letter.

14.   An en_____ sales representative can always find new sales outlets.

15.   There are 12 sa_____ members of staff here, and the rest work on a commission-only basis.

16.   She was in co_____ employment for the period 1998 - 2002.

17.   The co_____ committee was able to keep senior management in touch with feelings in the organisation.

18.   We have a st_____ lunch hour so that there is always someone on the switchboard.

© Bloomsbury Publishing Plc. For reference see *Dictionary of Human Resources and Personnel Management* (ISBN 0 7475 6623 2)

Adjectives 2

Complete each of these sentences with an adjective from the box. There is a dictionary definition of the word you will need after each sentence.

| able-bodied • acting • affiliated • aggrieved • capable • casual |
| discriminatory • eligible • generous • ~~impartial~~ • irregular • minimal |
| punctual • steady • voluntary |

---

1. The arbitration board's decision is completely _impartial_ *(not biased or not prejudiced)*

2. She is a very _____ departmental manager. *(efficient)*

3. There is a _____ demand for experienced computer programmers. *(continuing in a regular way)*

4. This procedure is highly _____. *(not correct, or not done in the correct way)*

5. The appointment of only males to the six posts was clearly _____. *(referring to the treatment of people in a different way because of race, age, sex, etc)*

6. Staff are only _____ for paid leave when they have been here for more than three months. *(allowed, or can be chosen)*

7. During our busy summer period, we employ _____ workers to deal with our extra orders. *(not permanent or regular)*

8. _____ workers should initially take any complaints to the Human Resources manager. *(upset and annoyed)*

9. The work is strenuous and only suitable for the young and _____. *(with no physical handicap)*

10. He's a very _____ employee who works extremely hard. *(tending to arrive at a place at the right time)*

11. The head office exercises _____ control over the branch offices. *(the smallest possible)*

12. Smiths Ltd is one of our _____ companies. *(connected with or owned by another company)*

13. We can use _____ workers to help in fund raising for charity. *(without being paid)*

14. If you leave now, we can offer you a _____ redundancy payment. *(referring to an amount that is larger than usual or expected)*

15. While Ms Henderson is on maternity leave, Mr Mullet will be _____ manager. *(working in place of someone for a short time)*

Also see: Wordbuilding 1: *Adjectives* on page 9
              Wordbuilding 4: *Opposites* on page 13

© Bloomsbury Publishing Plc. For reference see *Dictionary of Human Resources and Personnel Management* (ISBN 0 7475 6623 2)

Wordbuilding 1: Adjectives

Complete these sentences with an *adjective* formed from the verb in **bold**. Do this by adding a suffix (e.g. *-able*, *-ous*, *-ful*, etc) to the verb. In some cases, you will also need to remove letters, or add other letters. The first one has been done for you.

1.   Production has been slow because of _continual_ machine breakdowns on the shop floor.
      continue

2.   To qualify for paid leave, you need to have been in _____ employment for at least three months without a break. **continue**

3.   During my appraisal, my manager made some very _____ comments. **construct**

4.   To do well in this line of work, you need to be _____ and _____. **create / compete**

5.   The effect of the change in our discount structure is not _____. **quantify**

6.   If you look at the company's poor performance last year, this year has been a _____ success. **compare**

7.   His main complaint is that he finds the work _____ and _____. **bore / repeat**

8.   It's very important to be _____ in a job like this. **decide**

9.   I wouldn't like to offer them a contract because I don't think they're very _____. **depend**

10.   I'm afraid your work hasn't been very _____ this year. **satisfy**

11.   He gets _____ treatment because he's the MD's son. **prefer**

12.   The work she does is extremely _____. **admire**

13.   The agency was _____, but refused to refund our fee. **apologise**

14.   Because of excessive down time, it's _____ whether we'll achieve our production targets this month. **doubt**

15.   We are _____ that the company will accept our offer. **hope**

16.   Work-related injuries often occur because workers aren't _____ enough. **care**

17.   There are a lot of _____ mistakes in this report. **care**

18.   He's a very _____ person to work with. **agree**

19.   Although she retired last year, she still plays an _____ role in the company. **act**

20.   Each member of staff has to pass an _____ medical test. **oblige**

21.   Heart attacks are one of the _____ hazards of directors. **occupy**

22.   She doesn't work here full-time, but plays a _____ role in the running of the company.
      consult

23.   This post offers an _____ salary and a large benefits package. **attract**

24.   We had to readvertise the job because there were no _____ candidates. **suit**

25.   The sales manager is completely _____. **rely**

9

© Bloomsbury Publishing Plc. For reference see *Dictionary of Human Resources and Personnel Management* (ISBN 0 7475 6623 2)

Wordbuilding 2: Nouns 1

Look at the *verbs* in **bold** in the first sentence of each pair, and change them to nouns in the second sentence by changing the end of the word. There is an example at the beginning.

1.   The company will **compensate** the worker for the burns he suffered in the accident.
     The worker will receive   _compensation_   for the burns he suffered in the accident.

2.   The company tried to **motivate** its employees by promising bonus payments.
     The company tried to increase its employees _____ by promising bonus payments.

3.   How are the jobs in this organization **classified**?
     What are the job _____ in this organization?

4.   They **argued** about the price.
     They had an _____ about the price.

5.   My secretary leaves us next week, so we will need someone to **replace** her.
     My secretary leaves us next week, so will need to find a _____ for her.

6.   The personnel director has to **sign** the contract of employment.
     The personnel director's _____ has to go on the contract of employment.

7.   We have **agreed** the terms of the contract.
     We have come to an _____ on the terms of the contract.

8.   He told us that he had been **promoted** from salesman to sales manager.
     He told us about his _____ from salesman to sales manager.

9.   You should **apply** for the post as soon as possible.
     You should get your _____ for the job in as soon as possible.

10. No one has **authorised** him to act on our behalf.
     No one has given him _____ to act on our behalf.

11. Everyone congratulated him when he was **appointed** to the post of manager.
     Everyone congratulated him on his _____ to the post of manager.

12. Mr Smith was **succeeded** as chairman by Mrs Jones.
     Mr Smith's _____ as chairman was Mrs Jones.

13. Last year she **qualified** as an accountant.
     Last year she received her accountancy _____.

© Bloomsbury Publishing Plc. For reference see *Dictionary of Human Resources and Personnel Management* (ISBN 0 7475 6623 2)

14. This document **permits** you to export twenty-five computer systems.
    The document gives you _____ to export twenty-five computer systems.

15. The supervisor keeps a record of whether or not staff **attend** meetings.
    The supervisor keeps a record of staff _____ at meetings.

16. Does the contract we have produced **satisfy** the client?
    Does the contract we have produced meet with the client's _____?

17. The negotiations **failed** because neither side would compromise.
    The _____ of the negotiations was due to neither side reaching a compromise.

18. They are **negotiating** his new contract.
    His new contract is under _____.

19. We haven't received his letter **accepting** the job we offered him.
    We haven't received his letter of _____ for the job we offered him.

20. She asked the union to **intervene** on her behalf.
    She asked for the union's _____ on her behalf.

21. The employees have claimed that they were **dismissed** unfairly.
    The employees claim unfair _____.

22. The factory **consumes** a lot of water.
    The factory is a heavy _____ of water.

23. We **contend** that the decision of the tribunal is wrong.
    It is our _____ that the decision of the tribunal is wrong.

24. All companies should **insure** against loss of earnings.
    All companies should have _____ against loss of earnings.

25. Unless your work **improves**, we will have to review you position in the company.
    Unless we see an _____ in your work, we will have to review your position in the company.

26. By offering higher salaries, we might **entice** workers from other companies to join us.
    Offering higher salaries might be an _____ for workers from other companies to join us.

Wordbuilding 3: Nouns 2

Look at the *adjectives* in **bold** in the first sentence of each pair, and decide if the word in bold in the second sentence is the correct *noun* form of that adjective. If it is wrong, change it so that it is correct. The first one has been done as an example.

1. I am **responsible** for the welfare of the workers in my department.
   I have overall **responsibleness** for the welfare of the workers in my department.

   Wrong. The correct word is **responsibility**

2. The managing director is totally **confident** that the turnover will increase rapidly.
   The managing director has total **confidentiality** in the turnover increasing rapidly.

3. The chairman questioned whether she was **eligible** to stand for re-election.
   The chairman questioned her **eligibility** to stand for re-election.

4. They remarked that the sales director was **incompetent**.
   They remarked on the **incompetential** of the sales director.

5. The company's pricing policy is not **flexible**.
   There is no **flexibleness** in the company's pricing policy.

6. As a non-profit making organisation, we are **exempt** from paying taxes.
   As a non-profit making organisation, we can claim tax **exemptiality**.

7. Being physically **disabled** is not considered a disadvantage in this company.
   Physical **disablence** is not considered a disadvantage in this company.

8. The report criticized the sales staff as being **inefficient**.
   The report criticized the **inefficiency** of the sales staff.

9. In what way is a junior manager **different** from a managerial assistant?
   What's the **differention** between a junior manager and a managerial assistant?

10. Could you call us as soon as it is **convenient** for you?
    Could you call us at your earliest **convenientity**.

11. The manager wasn't **sympathetic** to her staff who complained of being overworked.
    The manager had no **sympatheticness** for her staff who complained of being overworked.

12. Everybody said how **accurate** the plans were.
    Everyone commented on the **accuration** of the plans.

13. She's a very **capable** manager.
    She has very good managerial **capablence**.

14. This test will help us to assess how **intelligent** the candidates are.
    This test will help us to assess the candidates' **intelligentness**.

15. The aim of the advertising campaign is to keep customers **loyal**.
    The aim of the advertising campaign is to keep customer **loyalty**.

Wordbuilding 4: Opposites

Change the *adjectives* in **bold** to their opposite form using a prefix. The first one has been done as an example.

The prefixes you will need are: *dis-   il-   im-   in-   ir-   un-.*

1. **Direct** taxes are taxes that are not paid direct to the government.
    = *Indirect*

2. The manager's treatment of the clerk was **fair** and completely **justified**.

3. **Efficient** workers waste raw materials and fail to complete tasks on schedule.

4. Her views and those of the department manager were **compatible**.

5. The company was criticized for operating with **adequate** cover.

6. This procedure is highly **regular**, and you mustn't do it again.

7. The job offer was **conditional**, and he accepted it immediately.

8. She seems to be **capable** of arriving on time.

9. The strike was **official**, and according to management it was also **legal**.

10. He is too **decisive** to be a good manager.

11. The debt is **recoverable**, so we have decided to write it off.

12. You are **eligible** for paid sick leave until you have worked here for three months.

13. I'm afraid we're rather **satisfied** with your work.

14. The negotiating team was quite **experienced** in dealing with management negotiators.

15. '**Effective** time' is the time spent by a worker which does not contribute to production.

16. The terms of the contract are quite **acceptable**.

17. The sales manager is **competent** and we should consider looking for someone new.

18. The company was declared **solvent** when it could no longer pay its debts.

19. The company has several **tangible** fixed assets, including copyrights and trademarks.

20. You are **authorised** to make major decisions without first consulting the directors.

21. Getting skilled staff is becoming **possible**.

22. Under the terms of your contract, you can be dismissed for **reasonable** behaviour.

Prepositions

The sentences in this exercise contain mistakes. The mistakes are all in the prepositions and there are three types:

1. A missing preposition
   *Example: I spoke him about this last week = I spoke **to** him about this last week.*
2. A wrong preposition
   *Example: We're meeting again in Tuesday = We're meeting again **on** Tuesday.*
3. An unnecessary preposition
   Example: I'll telephone to you tomorrow = I'll telephone ~~to~~ you tomorrow.

Find the mistakes and correct them.

1.   Six of the management trainees have been sponsored their companies.

2.   The chairman is abroad in business.

3.   Several members of staff were made redundant under the recession.

4.   His background is the electronics industry.

5.   The company will meet to your expenses.

6.   She wrote a letter of complaint the manager.

7.   The company enticed staff from other companies through offering them higher salaries.

8.   Although they threatened dismiss him, his performance at work didn't improve.

9.   Membership is by the discretion of the committee.

10. I have been granted with compassionate leave to visit a sick relative.

11. The new assistant manager has a degree on Business Studies.

12. Some of our staff work up to ten hours for every day.

13. She is away with maternity leave.

14. We still have to overcome on several obstacles in our negotiations with the union.

15. My salary is equivalent that of far less experienced employees in other organisations.

16. Employees have noticed on an improvement in the working environment.

17. He is under full-time employment.

18. There are no grounds of dismissal.

19. Insider trading is not only immoral, but it is also the law.

20. We're meeting the sales reps in London the day before tomorrow.

21. On the terms of your contract, you can't work for another company.

22. We rely our suppliers to make sure deliveries are made on time.

23. I would like to know who is responsible about causing all these problems.

24. If you can't work pressure, you will probably find the work very difficult.

25. After three years at university, she took out a job in a small printing firm.

26. I look forward hearing from you soon.

© Bloomsbury Publishing Plc. For reference see *Dictionary of Human Resources and Personnel Management* (ISBN 0 7475 6623 2)

This exercise lets you review some of the more common uses of 'grammar'-type words (prepositions, conjunctions, pronouns, prepositions, etc) in context. Use one word to complete each gap in the sentences. In some cases, more than one answer may be possible. There is an example at the beginning.

1. I enjoy working _with_ people who come _____ a wide range of backgrounds. _____ is the reason why I'm so keen _____ working in Human Resources.

2. 'Hands On', _____ is in the city centre, is _____ of the biggest employment agencies in _____ country.

3. A few years _____, people _____ to have the same career for life. _____ days, they can reasonably expect _____ change careers two _____ three times.

4. In spite _____ being rather lazy, he always _____ to get good results.

5. He spent _____ second year of his contract working in the Melbourne office, _____ he helped to double the sales figures.

6. _____ 2001 and 2005, the accession rate in this company increased _____ about 20% each year.

7. One _____ two of our employees commute from London, but _____ of them live _____ the office.

8. I'm afraid _____ say he has absolutely _____ chance _____ getting the job.

9. Staff are _____ allowed to leave early, _____ if they promise to work overtime _____ the weekend.

10. Please come _____ time to the meeting, and _____ prepared to stay late.

11. _____ you do really well in your attainment test, you _____ be asked to attend _____ retraining course.

12. We discussed holding the interviews _____ our Bristol branch, but _____ how many people _____ apply for the position, we decided to use our bigger offices _____ Birmingham.

13. In most respects he was a typical employee, but _____ made him different _____ everybody else in the company _____ his enthusiasm for working at weekends.

14. _____ least 60 people turned up for the presentation, which was far _____ than the organisers expected, and _____ there were only 20 chairs, most of us _____ to stand.

15. Managers are _____ capable of making mistakes as _____ else.

16. Pauline Halmsworth, a production manager _____ works in our Chicago department, has _____ received an 'Employee of the Year' award.

17. He approached the training course _____ enthusiasm, and _____ excellent progress as a result.

18. She worked for the company _____ the age of 26 _____ she retired, and during _____ time she only took one or two days _____ sick.

19. Her sudden change of heart took everyone _____ surprise, since previously she _____ been very interested in the project.

20. Reduction _____ demand has led _____ the cancellation _____ several new projects _____ we had hoped to implement.

© Bloomsbury Publishing Plc. For reference see *Dictionary of Human Resources and Personnel Management* (ISBN 0 7475 6623 2)

Formal words 1

In a business / office environment, we often use 'formal' words, especially in our written English (letters, reports, etc). For example, instead of 'asked for advice', we might use 'consulted'.

We **asked** our accountant **for advice** about our tax.
becomes:
We **consulted** our accountant about our tax.

These 'formal' words are often verbs.

Change the 'neutral' verbs and expressions in **bold** in these sentences to more 'formal' words using the verbs / expressions in the box. Each sentence requires only *one* word or expression. In most cases, you will need to change the form of the verb.

address •	adjourn •	adjust •	administer •	admonish •	advise
amalgamate •	analyse •	annul •	appeal to •	appoint •	apportion
assess at •	assign •	assist •	assure •	attend •	audit • avert
		await •	award		

1. We need to **examine in detail** the market potential of these new products.

2. The value of the business was **calculated to be** £5 million.

3. The management increased their offer in the hope of **stopping** the strike **happening**.

4. It will be the HR manager's job to **organise** the induction programme.

5. He was **given** the job of checking the sales figures.

6. The contract was **cancelled** by the court.

7. Our accountants have been asked to **examine** the accounts for the last quarter.

8. When he was dismissed, he **asked** his union **for support**.

9. The chairman **spoke to** the sales team.

10. At the meeting it was decided to **give** middle management a salary increase.

11. The workers were **given a warning** by the manager for careless work.

12. We are **waiting for** the decision of the planning department.

13. Prices will be **changed** according to the current rate of inflation.

14. The chairman **stopped** the meeting until 3 o'clock.

15. We have **chosen** a new distribution manager.

16. Production costs are **shared** according to projected revenue.

17. The chairman has asked all managers to **come to** the meeting.

18. We have been **told** that the shipment will arrive next week.

19. Can you **help** me with these income tax returns?

20 The different unions have **joined together to make one main union**.

© Bloomsbury Publishing Plc. For reference see *Dictionary of Human Resources and Personnel Management* (ISBN 0 7475 6623 2)

Formal words 2

The words and expressions in **bold** in the first of each pair of sentences can be replaced by a more 'formal' verb in the second sentence. These verbs can be found in the box below, but in most cases you will need to change their form.

Write your answers in the crossword grid on the next page.

| brief • consent • consult • dismiss • elect • engage • enter |
| index • inquire • license • notify • outline • present • redeploy |
| reinstate • retain • sequester • settle • specify • tender |
| undertake • upgrade • waive |

Across (⬌)

2. The management agreed to measures to **keep** experienced staff **in the company**.
   The management agreed to measures to _____ experienced staff.

6. The sales people were **told** about the new product in detail.
   The sales people were _____ about the new product.

7. The management **agreed** to the union's proposals.
   The management _____ to the union's proposals.

8. The union has had its funds **taken away by order of the courts**.
   The union has had its funds _____ .

12. The insurance company refused to **pay** his claim for storm damage.
   The insurance company refused to _____ his claim for storm damage.

15. The chairman **gave a general description of** the company's plans for the coming year.
   The chairman _____ the company's plans for the coming year.

17. The union demanded that the sacked workers should be **allowed to return to the jobs from which they were dismissed**.
   The union demanded that the sacked workers should be _____ .

18. After a lot of thought, he decided to **hand in** his resignation.
   After a lot of thought, he decided to _____ his resignation.

19. The court **refused to accept** his claim for compensation.
   The court _____ his claim for compensation.

20. If we increase production, we will need to **take on** more staff.
   If we increase production, we will need to _____ more staff.

21. Her job has been **increased in importance** to senior manager level.
   Her job has been _____ to senior manager level.

Down (⬇)

1. He has **given up** his right to early retirement.
   He has _____ his right to early retirement.

3. The management were **formally told** of the union's decision.
   The management were _____ of the union's decision.

4. The HR director will **talk about** the new staff structure to the Board.
   The HR director will _____ the new staff structure to the Board.

5. The union has **agreed** not to call a strike without further negotiation.
   The union has _____ not to call a strike without further negotiation.

© Bloomsbury Publishing Plc. For reference see *Dictionary of Human Resources and Personnel Management* (ISBN 0 7475 6623 2)

7. We **asked** our accountant **for advice** about our tax.
   We _____ our accountant about our tax.

8. Candidates are asked to **state clearly** which of the posts they are applying for.
   Candidates are asked to _____ which of the posts they are applying for.

9. He **chose** to take early retirement.
   He _____ to take early retirement.

10. We closed the design department and **moved** the workforce **to another department.**
    We closed the design department and _____ the workforce.

11. Salaries are **linked** to the cost of living.
    Salaries are _____ to the cost of living.

13. We are **trying to find out about** the background of the new supplier.
    We are _____ into the background of the new supplier.

14. The company has been **given formal permission** to sell spare parts.
    The company has been _____ to sell spare parts.

16. If you want to see the HR manager, **write** your name in the appointments book.
    If you want to see the HR manager, _____ your name in the appointments book.

© Bloomsbury Publishing Plc. For reference see *Dictionary of Human Resources and Personnel Management* (ISBN 0 7475 6623 2)

Word association 1

The four words in *italics* in each of these sentences can be linked by one other word. All these words have human resources connections. What are they? Write your answers in the grid at the bottom of the page (the first and last letters of each word have been done for you). If you do this correctly, you will reveal something in the shaded vertical strip that all candidates should have or prepare when they apply for a job.

1. This word can come <u>before</u> *accounting*, *analysis* and *factor*, and <u>after</u> *marginal*.

2. This word can come <u>before</u> *age*, *pay*, *wage* and *salary*.

3. This word can come <u>before</u> *review* and *structure*, and <u>after</u> *annual* and *basic*.

4. This word can come <u>before</u> *call* and *notice*, and <u>after</u> *unofficial* and *wildcat*.

5. This word can come <u>before</u> *transfer* and *work*, and <u>after</u> *evening* and *day*.

6. This word can come <u>before</u> *cover*, *examination*, *insurance* and *report*.

7. This word can come <u>before</u> *force* and *dispute*, and <u>after</u> *skilled* and *manual*.

8. This word can come <u>before</u> *agency* and *law*, and <u>after</u> *full-time* and *temporary*.

9. This word can come <u>before</u> *policy* and *cover*, and <u>after</u> *national* and *medical*.

10. This word can come <u>before</u> *tax* and *support*, and <u>after</u> *earned* and *net*.

11. This word can come <u>before</u> *enterprise*, *ownership*, *secretary* and *sector*.

12. This word can come <u>before</u> *scheme* and *contributions*, and <u>after</u> *occupational* and *portable*.

13. This word can come <u>before</u> *agency* and *appointment*, and <u>after</u> *senior* and *skeleton*.

14. This word can come <u>before</u> *work* and *law*, and <u>after</u> *fixed-term* and *under*.

15. This word can come <u>before</u> *allowance*, *assistant*, *contract* and *development*.

#												
1					C			T				
2	M					M						
3		S				Y						
4				S				E				
5				S			T					
6		M					L					
7		L				R						
8			E								T	
9			I						E			
10		I				E						
11			P					E				
12		P					N					
13				S			F					
14	C					T						
15				P							L	

© Bloomsbury Publishing Plc. For reference see *Dictionary of Human Resources and Personnel Management* (ISBN 0 7475 6623 2)

Word association 2

Link the verbs in sentences 1 - 15 with a noun from the box to make word 'partnerships'. The first one has been done as an example.

accounts •	an appointment •	a complaint •	a contract •	instructions
a job •	a pension •	a post •	qualifications •	redundancy • resignation
	rules •	a salary •	a tax •	~~work~~

1.   You can start, be in or out of, look for, offer or return to _work_ .

2.   You can follow, carry out, give, issue or receive _____.

3.   You can acquire, gain, hold, lack or need _____.

4.   You can announce, avoid, face, receive or take _____.

5.   You can draw, earn, offer, pay, raise, review or reduce _____.

6.   You can offer, negotiate, sign, break, terminate or renew _____.

7.   You can apply for, offer, create, accept, leave or turn down _____.

8.   You can make, arrange, schedule, confirm, keep or cancel _____.

9.   You can levy, impose, lift, deduct, raise or introduce _____.

10.   You can pay, settle, keep or falsify _____.

11.   You can announce, tender, demand, hand in, offer or accept _____.

12.   You can collect, pay into, draw, take out, qualify for or invest in _____.

13.   You can make, resolve, respond to, uphold, deal with, investigate or be cause for _____.

14.   You can break, enforce, obey, disobey, violate, bend, relax or comply with _____.

15.   You can apply for, offer, take up, hold, fill, be appointed to or accept _____.

© Bloomsbury Publishing Plc. For reference see *Dictionary of Human Resources and Personnel Management* (ISBN 0 7475 6623 2)

Word association 3

Part 1:

Identify the 13 words in this box by reading from left to right (▶) and from right to left (◀), following the directions of the arrows. The first one has been done for you as an example.

⇨	c	o	m	p	u	t	e	r	s	t	a	f	f	t	a	x	m	a	n	a	⇗
⇙	a	l	f	l	e	s	s	e	n	i	s	u	b	t	n	e	m	e	g	⇙
⇘	b	o	u	r	p	a	y	c	a	r	e	e	r	c	o	m	p	a	n	y	⇗
End	l	a	i	r	t	s	u	d	n	i	b	o	j	s	e	l	a	s	⇙

Part 2:

Each of the words above can be used before these groups of words. Decide which word can come before each group. Word group 10 has been done for you.

Group 1:
- comparability, day, differentials, freeze, hike, package, parity, rise, round, scale

Group 2:
- abatement, adjustment, allowance, bracket, code, credit, declaration, exemption, form, shelter, threshold

Group 3:
- audit, committee, course, development, education, function, ratio, style, team, technique, trainee

Group 4:
- application, ceiling, cuts, cycle, description, dissatisfaction, enlargement, enrichment, freeze, loading, offer, opportunities, rotation

Group 5:
- charges, dispute, force, grading, injunction, market, mobility, relations, turnover, wastage

Group 6:
- accident, action, development, disease, dispute, health, practices, relations, tribunal, unrest

Group 7:
- car, director, executive, handbook, law, loyalty, secretary, town, union

Group 8:
- analysis, assistant, budget, campaign, chart, department, drive, executive, force, manager, representative, target

Group 9:
- agency, appointment, association, canteen, incentives, management, outing, representative, status, turnover

Group 10:
- department, error, file, fraud, language, listing, literate, manager, programmer, readable, services, system   (**Answer = computer**)

Group 11:
- anchor, break, change, development, expectations, ladder, opportunities, path, pattern, structure, woman

Group 12:
- address, agent, card, centre, college, cycle, expenses, letter, plan, school

Group 13:
- appraisal, assessment, certification, confidence, employed, fulfilment, managed team, starter

© Bloomsbury Publishing Plc. For reference see *Dictionary of Human Resources and Personnel Management* (ISBN 0 7475 6623 2)

Word association 4: *salary* and *wage*

1.   Rearrange these letters to make adjectives that can come before *wage* and *salary*. The first letter of each word has been <u>underlined</u>.

ba<u>l</u>elevi   gini<u>l</u>v   ca<u>b</u>is   moi<u>n</u>nla   iuim<u>m</u>mn   hony<u>m</u>tl   graeve<u>a</u>   alnu<u>a</u>n   eyy<u>r</u>la

2.   Complete this paragraph with verbs from the box.

| command • cut • dock • draw • earn • |
| fall • offer • pay • raise • rise • reduce |

An employee can (a) _____ or (b) _____ a wage or salary. An employer can (c)_____, (d)_____, (e)_____, (f)_____ or (g)_____ salaries or wages. If an employee is persistently late or does something wrong, the employer can (h)_____ his wages. Wages and salaries can (i)_____ or (j)_____. An experienced worker who is in great demand can (k)_____ a high wage or salary from a new employer.

3.   Decide whether these statements are *true* or *false*:

(a) Changes made to wages are called *wage adjustments*.

(b) The basis on which an employee is paid is called a *wage formation*.

(c) A *wage-price spiral* occurs when prices fall, and so wages fall as well.

(d) The act of keeping increases in wages under control is called a *wage restraint*.

(e) A *wage freeze* is a period during which a company doesn't pay any wages.

(f) The differences in wages between employees in similar types of jobs are called *wage differences*.

(g) A *wages floor* is the department in a company which is responsible for paying the employees

(h) A financial benefit offered as a reward to employees who perform very well is called a *wage incentive*.

4.   Complete these dictionary definitions with words from the box.

| bands • ceiling • cut • deductions • drift |
| expectations • review • structure |

(a) Salary _____ refers to money which a company removes from salaries to pay to the government as tax, National Insurance, etc.

(b) A salary _____ is the organisation of salaries in a company with different rates of pay for different jobs.

(c) Salary _____ is a situation where an increase in pay is greater than that of officially negotiated rates.

(d) Salary _____ are the hopes of an employee that their salary will increase.

(e) A salary _____ is a re-examination by an employer of an employee's pay.

(f) A salary _____ is the highest level on a pay scale that an employee can achieve under his or her contract.

g) Salary _____ are all the salaries at different levels in a company.

(h) A salary _____ is a sudden reduction in salary.

Word association 5: *work* and *working*

A. Hidden in the grid below there are 23 words that can be used after *work* and *working*? How many can you find? You can find them by reading across (➧) and down (⬇).

For example: *work profiling* *working supervisor*

s	s	e	x	p	e	r	i	e	n	c	e	o	h	s	i	s
h	t	t	d	a	y	a	b	c	d	e	f	u	g	c	p	t
a	a	h	o	u	r	s	r	a	g	e	l	t	j	h	r	r
d	n	i	l	c	o	n	d	i	t	i	o	n	s	e	o	u
o	d	c	u	t	e	a	m	k	l	m	w	n	o	d	f	c
w	a	p	n	s	u	p	e	r	v	i	s	o	r	u	i	t
p	r	a	c	t	i	c	e	s	q	l	o	a	d	l	l	u
r	d	s	h	o	v	e	r	l	o	a	d	t	u	e	i	r
m	e	a	s	u	r	e	m	e	n	t	v	w	x	o	n	i
y	s	h	a	r	i	n	g	s	a	m	p	l	i	n	g	n
w	e	e	k	z	s	t	o	p	p	a	g	e	a	b	c	g

B. Use the expressions to complete these sentences.

1. Everybody in the office is suffering from stress because there's so much to do all the time. They're all complaining of ________.
2. The factory is noisy, dark, hot and dirty. The union says that unless ________ improve, they'll down tools and walk out.
3. According to our ________ figures, it should be possible for a team of five skilled employees to produce 20 units an hour.
4. Fiona's a student on a business course. She's spending some time with our company on ________ to see how a successful company is run.
5. My ________ are from nine to five, but I get 30 minutes for lunch, and two 20-minute breaks.
6. Karen is our ________: she works on the production line, but she also controls the work of the others on the factory floor.
7. I resigned last week, but I need to ________ my notice, so I'll be here for another 3 weeks.
8. ________ is becoming increasingly common as people have to do more in less time, with inadequate equipment and in an unpleasant environment. There have even been reports of physical violence.
9. The company has made radical changes in its ________ recently in an attempt to increase production and create a more flexible working environment.
10. According to our ________ for today, we need to have 500 units checked, packed and despatched by lunchtime.
11. We're going to have a busy day, with meetings all morning, a staff development workshop in the afternoon, and a ________ in-between.
12. Frequent ________ by the union are holding up production and losing us money.

© Bloomsbury Publishing Plc. For reference see *Dictionary of Human Resources and Personnel Management* (ISBN 0 7475 6623 2)

Two-word expressions 1

Exercise 1

Complete the words in the grid to make two-word expressions connected with Human Resources. You have been given the first letter of each word, and you can find the rest of each word in the box below the grid. The first one has been done as an example.

a _ccession_ rate	b_____ scheme	c_____ provision
d_____ action	e_____ liability	f_____ worker
g_____ procedure	h_____ capital	i_____ plan
j_____ satisfaction	k_____-how	l_____ manager
m_____ round	n_____ assessment	o_____ mobility
p_____ ladder	q_____ time	r_____ rate
s_____ differential	t_____ spirit	u_____ communication
v_____ redundancy	w_____ dismissal	y_____-man

_ccession • _ccupational • _eam • _eeds • _eplacement • _es _hift • _hildcare • _ilk • _ine • _isciplinary • _mployer's • _ncentive • _now • _ob • _oluntary • _onus • _pward • _reelance _rievance • _romotion • _rongful • _uality • _uman

Exercise 2

Complete these sentences with a two-word expression from above.

1. _____ _____ had to be taken to prevent further disputes between workers and managers.

2. In return for a large payment, several of our employees have offered to accept _____ _____.

3. We will begin the recruitment drive with our annual _____ _____, beginning at North London University.

4. We have to carry out a _____ _____ so that we can decide which of our employees should go for further training, and which should be transferred.

5. These days, it is not enough to be able to do one job well. You need to have _____ _____ so that you can more from job to job effectively.

6. Our _____ _____ is £7.50 an hour, but this rises to £10.50 an hour after the employee has been with us for six months.

7. By being appointed sales manager, she moved several steps up the _____ _____.

8. If you want to be successful in this company, it's important to acquire a bit of computer _____ _____ and other IT skills.

9. When she was sacked for sending personal emails when she should have been working, she complained of _____ _____ to her union.

10. This company has a very high _____ _____, which many of our employees are blaming on poor management.

© Bloomsbury Publishing Plc. For reference see *Dictionary of Human Resources and Personnel Management* (ISBN 0 7475 6623 2)

Two-word expressions 2

Hidden in the two boxes below there are 39 expressions which use two words. The first word of each expression can be found in the first box, and the second word can be found in the second box. The words can be found by reading from left to right (◗) only. Set yourself a time limit of 10 minutes to see how many you can find. One word in the second box can be used twice.

Examples: *track record*   *body language*

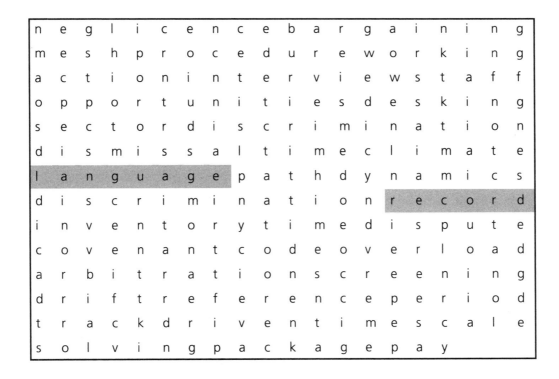

a	d	v	e	r	s	e	a	d	v	i	s	o	r	y	g	r	o	u	p
a	g	e	h	e	a	l	t	h	r	e	s	t	r	i	c	t	i	v	e
r	a	c	i	a	l	t	e	r	t	i	a	r	y	c	a	r	e	e	r
s	e	v	e	r	a	n	c	e	t	r	a	c	k	r	e	s	u	l	t
n	e	g	l	i	g	e	n	t	h	o	t	o	f	f	i	c	i	a	l
i	n	e	f	f	e	c	t	i	v	e	i	m	m	e	d	i	a	t	e
i	n	c	r	e	m	e	n	t	a	l	a	p	p	r	a	i	s	a	l
c	o	l	l	a	b	o	r	a	t	i	v	e	p	r	o	b	l	e	m
i	n	f	o	r	m	a	t	i	o	n	s	k	i	l	l	s	s	e	x
v	a	l	u	e	g	r	o	s	s	a	t	t	e	n	d	a	n	c	e
a	l	l	o	w	e	d	c	o	r	p	o	r	a	t	e	f	a	s	t
b	o	d	y	c	o	l	l	e	c	t	i	v	e	r	e	w	a	r	d
e	a	r	n	i	n	g	s	j	o	b	s	e	l	e	c	t	i	o	n
a	n	c	i	l	l	a	r	y	n	o	t	i	c	e	d	r	e	s	s

n	e	g	l	i	c	e	n	c	e	b	a	r	g	a	i	n	i	n	g
m	e	s	h	p	r	o	c	e	d	u	r	e	w	o	r	k	i	n	g
a	c	t	i	o	n	i	n	t	e	r	v	i	e	w	s	t	a	f	f
o	p	p	o	r	t	u	n	i	t	i	e	s	d	e	s	k	i	n	g
s	e	c	t	o	r	d	i	s	c	r	i	m	i	n	a	t	i	o	n
d	i	s	m	i	s	s	a	l	t	i	m	e	c	l	i	m	a	t	e
l	a	n	g	u	a	g	e	p	a	t	h	d	y	n	a	m	i	c	s
d	i	s	c	r	i	m	i	n	a	t	i	o	n	r	e	c	o	r	d
i	n	v	e	n	t	o	r	y	t	i	m	e	d	i	s	p	u	t	e
c	o	v	e	n	a	n	t	c	o	d	e	o	v	e	r	l	o	a	d
a	r	b	i	t	r	a	t	i	o	n	s	c	r	e	e	n	i	n	g
d	r	i	f	t	r	e	f	e	r	e	n	c	e	p	e	r	i	o	d
t	r	a	c	k	d	r	i	v	e	n	t	i	m	e	s	c	a	l	e
s	o	l	v	i	n	g	p	a	c	k	a	g	e	p	a	y

Phrasal verbs 1

Complete the sentences with a verb so that each sentence contains a phrasal verb. Use these verbs to complete the crossword grid on the next page. The sentences in italics explain what each phrasal verb means. The verbs you need are in the box, but in many cases you will need to change their form (past simple, past participle or present participle).

All of the phrasal verbs can be found in the *Bloomsbury Dictionary of Human Resources and Personnel Management*.

back • cancel • carry • close • drag • fall • fight • fill
follow • get • go • hand • hold • make • opt • phase
run • set • sort • turn • weed • work

Across (▶)

3. The company is _____ **down** its London office. *(to shut a shop, factory or service for a long period or for ever)*

5. We'll pay you half now, and _____ **up** the difference next month. *(to pay extra so that a loss or difference is covered)*

6. She doesn't _____ **on** with her new boss. *(to be friendly or work well with someone)*

8. Negotiations _____ **on** into the night. *(to continue slowly without ending)*

12. The unions are _____ **against** the proposed redundancies. *(to struggle to try to overcome something)*

14. I'll _____ **up** your idea of targeting our address list with a special mailing. *(to examine something further)*

16. Two months later, they _____ **back** on their agreement. *(not to do what has been promised)*

17. The company was _____ **up** in 1994. *(to begin something or to organise something new)*

18. He _____ **down** the job he was offered. *(to refuse)*

21. Discussion of item 4 was _____ **over** until the next meeting. *(to postpone or put back to a later date)*

22. In the last six months we have _____ **behind** our rivals. *(to have fewer sales or make less profit)*

Down (▼)

1. He decided to resign, so _____ **in** his notice. *(to deliver a letter by hand)*

2. He resigned last week, and is now _____ **out** his notice. *(to work during the time between resigning and actually leaving the company)*

4. The test is designed to _____ **out** candidates who have low mathematical skills. *(to remove unsuitable candidates or employees)*

7. The staff _____ **on** working in spite of the fire. *(to continue or to go on doing something)*

9. Higher costs have _____ **out** the increased sales revenue. *(to balance or act against each other and so make each other invalid)*

10. I'll _____ **in** for him while he is away at his brother's wedding. *(to do someone else's job temporarily)*

11. Smith Ltd will be _____ **out** as a supplier of spare parts. *(to remove something gradually)*

13. Did you _____ **out** the accounts problem with the auditor? *(to put into order)*

15. Do you think they'll _____ **out** when they realise how hard the project is? *(to decide not to do something)*

19. Your suggestions sound good. Let's _____ **with** them for a while. *(informal - to decide to carry out an idea or project)*

20. His union refused to _____ him **up** in his argument with management. *(to support or help)*

© Bloomsbury Publishing Plc. For reference see *Dictionary of Human Resources and Personnel Management* (ISBN 0 7475 6623 2)

Phrasal verbs 2

Each sentence 1 - 12 can be completed with a phrasal verb, using a verb and a particle or particles from boxes A + B. Write the appropriate phrasal verb for each sentence in the grid. In some cases you will need to change the form of the verb.

If you do it correctly, you will reveal another phrasal verb in the shaded vertical strip. This phrasal verb means 'to make something happen earlier than originally planned'.

A: Use these verbs
break   bring   build   burn   fill   gear   get   give   hold   stand

B: Use these particles:
across   down   back   for   in   into   off   out   to   up   way

The sentences in *italics* after each sentence explain what the phrasal verb means.

1.   Payment will be _____ _____ until the contract has been signed. *(to wait, to not go forward)*

2.   The company is _____ itself _____ _____ expansion into the African market. *(to get ready)*

3.   You must _____ all the forecasts _____ the budget. *(to add something to something else that is being set up)*

4.   Mr Smith is _____ _____ _____ the chairman, who is ill. *(to take someone's place)*

5.   At the meeting, the chairman _____ _____ the subject of redundancy payments. *(to refer to something for the first time)*

6.   Make sure you don't make any mistakes when you _____ _____ the application form. *(to write the required information in the spaces on a form)*

7.   He has _____ _____ the same job for the last six years. *(to manage to do a difficult job, usually over a long period of time)*

8.   Don't work too hard or you'll _____ yourself _____. *(to become tired and incapable of further work because of stress)*

9.   The management _____ _____ _____ the union's demands. *(to make concessions or agree to demands)*

10.   We weren't able to _____ _____ the discussions until midnight. *(to stop)*

11.   The manager tried to _____ _____ to the workforce why some people were being made redundant. *(to make someone understand something)*

12.   There isn't enough work, so we have to _____ some of you _____ for the day. *(to reduce employee's hours of work because of shortage of work)*

© Bloomsbury Publishing Plc. For reference see *Dictionary of Human Resources and Personnel Management* (ISBN 0 7475 6623 2)

Match the questions on the left with the most appropriate answers on the right. The answers contain a definition or an explanation of the phrasal verbs in **bold** on the left. The first one has been done for you.

1.	Would you **advise against** moving the head office to Edinburgh?
2.	Did you manage to **turn** the company **round**?
3.	Do you think the staff will **walk out** when they hear the news?
4.	Did you manage to **get through** to the complaints department?
5.	Shall we **put back** the meeting until everyone can come?
6.	Were the management willing to **improve on** their previous offer?
7.	Would you be prepared to **hold out** for a 10% pay rise?
8.	Will we be able to **hold** him **to** the contract?
9.	Can we **clock off** yet?
10.	Have you **taken over** the company?
11.	Are they hoping to **build up** a profitable business?
12.	Do you think you'll have to **let** Mr Walton **go**?
13.	Have our reps **called in** to give us their sales figures?
14.	Have the managers agreed to **take on** more staff for the Witney office?
15.	Can we **get along** all right with only half the staff we had before?

A.	Yes, they thought they might be able to do a bit better as long as we were prepared to work harder.
B.	Well, we haven't actually bought it yet, but we've made an offer to buy most of the shares.
C.	No, I don't think we're going to employ anyone else for the time being.
D.	Yes, I don't think we should do that.
E.	Possibly, but we're not sure we'd want to wait too long before asking.
F.	Yes, I've had three phone calls already this afternoon.
G.	Well, there has already been some gradual expansion, but it's going to take time.
H.	Well, I certainly think it's a good idea to move it to a later date.
I.	Yes, it was making a loss, but now it's a very profitable organisation.
J.	I hope so. I don't want to allow any changes to be made at this stage.
K.	We should manage, although everyone will have to work a bit harder.
L.	Yes, it's time to leave. Let's go home.
M.	Probably, and we really don't want everyone to stop working and leave in protest.
N.	We don't like making people redundant, but it looks like it's our only option.
O.	No, they weren't answering the phone.

Phrasal verbs 4

The following sentences each contain a phrasal verb in **bold**. However, half of them use the wrong phrasal verb. Decide which ones are wrong and replace them with the correct phrasal verb, which you will find in the other sentences. The phrasal verb you need for each sentence is explained in *italics* at the end of each sentence.

1.   If you complain, you might **get** your money **back**. *(to receive something which you had before)*

2.   The company was **broken up** and separate divisions sold off. *(to split something large into small sections)*

3.   If you want to **put out** in your job, you'll need to show more commitment. *(to advance in your career)*

4.   Payment will be **held up** until the contract has been signed. *(to delay)*

5.   We have installed networked computers to **cut down on** paperwork. *(to reduce the amount of something used)*

6.   Negotiations between management and the unions **backed out** after six hours. *(to stop a negotiation, usually because no agreement has been made)*

7.   We plan to **bring out** a new model of the car for the motor show. *(to produce something new)*

8.   She decided to take early retirement, so **took up** her responsibilities to her deputy. *(to pass your work responsibilities to someone else)*

9.   The accounts department **got out** the draft accounts in time for the meeting. *(to produce something)*

10.   After an agreement was reached, the union **phased in** the strike. *(to ask for something to stop)*

11.   The management have refused to **give up** pressure from the unions. *(to yield or to surrender)*

12.   The new system of pension contributions will be **called off** over the next two months. *(to introduce or bring something in gradually)*

13.   We may decide to **bring down** the price of some of our brands to help increase demand. *(to reduce)*

14.   After several years with the company, she **handed over** a new post with one of our competitors. *(to start a new job)*

15.   We had to cancel the project when our German partners **broke down**. *(to stop being a part of a deal or arrangement)*

16.   Workers refused to **give in to** any of their rights. *(to hand something to someone, or to lose something, often as the result of pressure from someone)*

17.   The meeting has been **put off** for two weeks. *(to arrange for something to take place later than planned)*

18.   We are planning to **get ahead** most of our work to freelancers. *(to send or give a job to someone else, usually not in your company)*

19.   He **got on** well in his new job, and was soon promoted. *(to succeed)*

20.   It's very important to **carry out** your duties to the best of your ability. *(to do what is necessary for your job)*

© Bloomsbury Publishing Plc. For reference see *Dictionary of Human Resources and Personnel Management* (ISBN 0 7475 6623 2)

Idioms 1: The people you work with

There are a lot of informal, idiomatic and slang words that we can use to talk about different types of people who work in a company. Many of them are used in a humorous way. Some of them are *not* very complimentary, so you should be careful how you use them!

Read the descriptions of these different people, then match them with the idiomatic noun in the box at the bottom of the page that best applies to them. The first one has been done for you.

1. Alice enjoys her work, and has no grievances against her employer. **= *a happy camper***

2. Brian is a brilliant young man who has quickly become very successful.

3. Clarice is an angry worker who is always spreading discontent in the office.

4. Daniel was brought in to deal with a big project, made a lot of fuss, achieved nothing and then left.

5. Elizabeth is a second-level manager who is responsible for carrying out commands and communicating messages from the top-level executives.

6. Frank works all the time, and is unhappy when he's not working.

7. Gary is new to our company, but he didn't need to be trained for the job as he was already experienced in his line of work.

8. Harriet is a junior executive who assists a senior executive, and is always following him around the building.

9. Ian is rich and successful because of all the hard work he has done.

10. Janine often moves from one job to another because she has skills that a lot of companies value.

11. Kevin is obsessed with the Internet, and spends all his time on the computer.

12. Louise is an influential and dynamic woman who makes things happen.

13. Martin always agrees with everything his boss says.

14. Nora secretly has a second job which she goes to in the evening, and which pays cash.

15. Oliver does a large variety of small jobs in the office.

16. Penelope always appears to have an endless supply of good ideas.

17. Richard is a senior executive who performs extremely well.

18. Sally left the company last year, but returned to work for us again last month.

19. Tom is an executive who dresses well and follows procedure, but doesn't actually contribute much to the company.

20. Ursula is a lazy employee who tries to get away with doing the least possible amount of work.

21. Vic is very knowledgeable about technology and mathematics, but is not very good at relating to people.

22. Wendy always follows her instincts when responding to a question rather than considering it rationally.

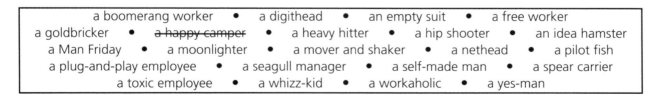

a boomerang worker • a digithead • an empty suit • a free worker
a goldbricker • a happy camper • a heavy hitter • a hip shooter • an idea hamster
a Man Friday • a moonlighter • a mover and shaker • a nethead • a pilot fish
a plug-and-play employee • a seagull manager • a self-made man • a spear carrier
a toxic employee • a whizz-kid • a workaholic • a yes-man

All of the words and expressions in this box can be found in the *Bloomsbury Dictionary of Human Resources and Personnel Management*.

Idioms 2

Choose the correct idiomatic word or expression in (a), (b), (c) or (d), for each of these sentences. You will find all the correct expressions in the *Bloomsbury Dictionary of Human Resources and Personnel Management*.

1. Boring and detailed work, such as examining documents for mistakes, could be described as:
   (a) **hammer and chisel work**   (b) **nut and bolt work**   (c) **bucket and spade work**
   (d) **pick and shovel work**

2. We sometimes say that people who compete for success in business or in a career are working for the:
   (a) **horse race**   (b) **dog race**   (c) **rat race**   (d) **camel race**

3. The practice of transferring a difficult, incompetent or non-essential employee from one department to another is known informally as a:
   (a) **weasel waltz**   (b) **turkey trot**   (c) **cat calypso**   (d) **rabbit rumba**

4. We might refer to a bad employer with a reputation for losing talented staff as a:
   (a) **people churner**   (b) **people mixer**   (c) **people stirrer**   (d) **people beater**

5. A job that is normally done by a woman, especially a young one, is sometimes referred to as:
   (a) **a pink-collar job**   (b) **a woolly-jumper job**   (c) **a fluffy-slipper job**   (d) **a furry-mule job**

6. If you do a lot of different types of work in an office for very low pay, you could be referred to as a:
   (a) **catsbody**   (b) **pigsbody**   (c) **ratsbody**   (d) **dogsbody**

7. When an employee telephones to say that s/he is not coming to work because s/he is ill, but in fact is only pretending to be ill, we say that s/he is taking or throwing a/an:
   (a) **unwellie**   (b) **illie**   (c) **horriblie**   (d) **sickie**

8. If an employee gets very angry at work because of something bad or unpleasant that happens, we can say that they are experiencing:
   (a) **office anger**   (b) **work rage**   (c) **shopfloor strops**   (d) **workplace wobblies**

9. If an employee is deliberately or accidentally excluded from decision-making processes, they might complain that they are being left:
   (a) **out of their mind**   (b) **out of the blue**   (c) **out of their head**   (d) **out of the loop**

10. Work that offers the same money for less effort than another similar job is often known as:
    (a) **a cushy number**   (b) **a doddle**   (c) **a pushover**   (d) **child's play**

11. When somebody is dismissed from their job, we can say that they have:
    (a) **got the shoe**   (b) **got the sandal**   (c) **got the boot**   (d) **got the slipper**

12. If you criticize somebody in writing, we can say that you _____ them.
    (a) **pencil-smack**   (b) **pencil-thrash**   (c) **pencil-punch**   (d) **pencil-whip**

Look at these mini-dialogues, and complete each one with an idiomatic expression from the box. You do not need to use all of the expressions.

cherry pick	•	dead wood	•	dress-down day	• dumbsizing • ear candy
exploding bonus	•	eye service	•	glad-hand	• graveyard shift • helicopter view
kiss up to	•	leaky reply	•	marzipan employee	• mushroom job
shape up or ship out	•	sweetener	•	three-martini lunch	

1. A. Oh no! Elaine sent me an email complaining about Mr Jones, and I wrote her a reply. I agreed that I thought Mr Jones was stupid and incompetent, and I've accidentally sent it to him!
    B. Oh well, don't worry. We all send a _____ now and then.

2. A. I've told Tom that unless he improves his performance at work, he'll be fired.
    B. Good. It's about time somebody told him to _____.

3. A. A lot of our factory employees are happy to work at night because the money is good.
    B. Yes, working the _____ can be a good way of making more money.

4. A. The only way to get promoted in this job is to flatter and be very attentive to the senior managers.
    B. That's terrible! You shouldn't have to _____ people to get ahead in your job.

5. A. We need to get rid of some of our older and less productive staff.
    B. I agree. The _____ has to go as soon as possible.

6. A. Ms Rigden met a lot of people at the conference, didn't she?
    B. She certainly did. I think I saw her _____ almost everyone there.

7. A. On Wednesdays, we're allowed to wear informal clothes to work.
    B. Us too. Our _____ is Friday.

8. A. My boss always compliments me and tells me how well I'm doing, but he never offers me a pay rise.
    B. Well, I suppose a bit of _____ is better than nothing.

9. A. A lot of people in out company only do any work when the supervisor is watching them.
    B. It's the same in our company. In fact, _____ is more common than you think.

10. A. We need to reduce the size of the company but we need to make sure it doesn't become unprofitable or inefficient.
    B. That's true. _____ is something we need to avoid at all costs.

11. A. Alan says he's thinking of leaving the company to work for someone else.
    B. That's not good news. Offer him a _____ and see if he can be persuaded to stay.

12. A. Do we need to look at all the problems in detail?
    B. No, not really. A _____ should be enough for now. We just need the main ideas.

© Bloomsbury Publishing Plc. For reference see *Dictionary of Human Resources and Personnel Management* (ISBN 0 7475 6623 2)

Changes

Exercise 1: Verbs

Complete these sentences with a verb from the box. In some cases, more than one answer may be possible. You will need to change the form of the verb in many cases. The first one has been done as an example.

adapt •	adjust •	alter •	decrease •	demote •	deteriorate •	downgrade
downsize •	enforce •	expand •	increase •	lay off •	phase in •	promote
redeploy •	reduce •	relax •	release •	relocate •	renew •	renovate
		replace •	retire •	~~streamline~~		

1. In order to _streamline_ distribution services, we are installing a new, more efficient computer system.

2. Because of her excellent work, she will be _____ from salesperson to manager.

3. The company will close for two weeks while the offices are being _____.

4. The good news this year is that company profits have _____ faster than the rate of inflation.

5. His contract was initially for five years, but it has recently been _____ for another three years.

6. When I wanted to leave the company early, the management refused to _____ me from my contract.

7. Older staff are being encouraged to _____ early.

8. We closed the design department and _____ the workforce to the publicity department.

9. We have _____ our sales force in order to cope with the extra demand for our products.

10. The company has decided to _____ the company rules on dress codes: from now on, office staff are not required to wear suits.

11. Our share of the domestic market has been much bigger since imports _____.

12. The company has decided to _____ the rules on smoking: from now on, anyone caught smoking on company premises will be fined.

13. He was _____ from manager to salesperson because of his poor handling of the department.

14. Over the next two years, we will _____ all our salaried staff with freelancers.

15. The quality of work in the office has _____ badly since the old manager left.

16. Salaries will be _____ to bring them in line with the higher rate of inflation.

17. We must _____ expenditure if we want to stay in business.

18. The new system of pension contributions will be _____ over the next two months.

19. The staff are finding it hard to _____ to the new style of management.

20. Because of poor demand for our products, we have had to _____ 20 workers.

21. When the company closed its London offices, the staff were _____ to other offices around the country.

22. Until recently the most senior position in the company was European Sales Manager, but this was _____ when the new post of International Sales Director was created.

23. In order to make the company more profitable, we have to _____ the workforce from 108 to about 60.

24. We need to _____ some of the terms of the contract before we make a final decision.

Exercise 2: Nouns

The verbs in the first box can also be nouns, or they can be made into nouns by changing the end of the word. Match the verbs with the instructions in the second box so that they become nouns. There is an example in the second box.

1. adjust •	2. alter •	3. decrease •	4. demote •	5. deteriorate
6. downgrade •	7. downsize •	8. enforce •	9. expand •	10. increase
11. promote •	12. redeploy •	13. reduce •	14. relax •	15. release
16. relocate •	17. renovate •	18. replace •	19. retire	

A.	No change (for example: *decrease*)
B.	Add **-ation**
C.	Remove **e** and add **-ing**
D.	Remove **e** and add **-ion**
E.	Add **-ment**
F.	Remove **d** and add **-sion**
G.	Remove **e** and add **-tion**

Over and under

Look at these mini-dialogues and complete each one with a word from the box. These words all include *over* or *under*. The first one has been done as an example for you. One word can be used twice.

---

overhaul • overheads • overmanned / overstaffed • overpaid
overqualified • overrated • overrule • overrun • overtime • overturn
overworked • underachiever • undermanned • undermine
understanding • understudy • undertaking • underutilised • ~~underworked~~

---

1.   A. The directors think that our staff are _underworked_ .
     B. Well, they are at the moment, but that's because demand for our products is so low.

2.   A. The workers have _____ the time limit set by the production manager.
     B. That's not good. They shouldn't go beyond the limits that set for them.

3.   A. We're rather _____ at the moment.
     B. Right. And unless the market improves, we might need to lay off some of our casual workers.

4.   A. Do you think our staff are _____?
     B. No, I don't. They work very hard for the money they receive.

5.   A. Everyone says that Elizabeth works hard, but in my opinion she's a bit of an _____.
     B. I agree. She doesn't do as much as she is capable.

6.   A. I'm learning how to do the production manager's job in case he needs to take some extended time off.
     B. Oh, I thought you were the _____ for the accounts manager.

7.   A. Does this business make a lot of money?
     B. Yes, it's a very profitable _____.

8.   A. Robert has a degree in business studies, doesn't he?
     B. Yes, so he's rather _____ to be an ordinary shop floor worker.

9.   A. Our sales revenue covers the manufacturing costs, but not the day-to-day running costs of the company.
     B. Right. We need to make sure we have enough to cover our _____.

10. A. Our staff are always complaining that they're _____.
     B. I don't know why. They get plenty of breaks, and most of them clock off before three o'clock.

© Bloomsbury Publishing Plc. For reference see *Dictionary of Human Resources and Personnel Management* (ISBN 0 7475 6623 2)

11.   A. Staff are worried that the director's complaints could _____ their productive ability.
        B. Well, perhaps they should call a meeting with the directors if they feel that their ability could be weakened.

12.   A. Apparently the management are going to _____ some of the decisions they made last month.
        B. Well I'm not sure they can cancel decisions that have already been made.

13.   A. The union and management decided to make some important changes last month, but the directors decided they couldn't go ahead with them.
        B. Are they allowed to _____ changes that have been mutually agreed?

14.   A. Our new computer system is excellent, but it's being _____.
        B. If it's not being used enough, perhaps it's because staff don't know how to use it.

15.   A. Do you think it's time we made a few changes to the way we run the company?
        B. Yes. The first thing we should do is to _____ the company's union agreements.

16.   A. We need a legally-binding promise that your workers will remain on the shop floor during negotiations.
        B. Fine, we'll provide you with a written _____ not to strike during that period.

17.   A. What's our current _____ rate?
        B. Well, if you work for more than the normal working time, it's one and a half times normal pay.

18.   A. We're worried that the department will be _____ during the Christmas period.
        B. If we don't have enough staff then, we can employ some casual workers.

19.   A. I think the 'first class service' they offer is valued more highly than it should be.
        B. I agree. It's vastly _____.

20.   A. The management and the union have come to an _____ about the demarcation problems.
        B. I don't think a private agreement is good enough. We need to have it in writing.

© Bloomsbury Publishing Plc. For reference see *Dictionary of Human Resources and Personnel Management* (ISBN 0 7475 6623 2)

A career case history

Part 1

In this text, you have been given the first two letters of some missing words and expressions. You will find the other parts of the words in the box. The first one has been done for you.

—lked out • —tire • —senteeism • —bezzlement • —gh achiever
—nd in • —ck • —smissed • —tice • —fered • —lled in
—op floor • —omoted • —ply for • —terview • —signed
—mmute • —plication form • —y off • —tend

Ian Woodham left college and decided to 1. **ap** _ply for_ a job which he saw advertised in the local paper. He 2. **fi**_____ the 3. **ap**_____ that the company sent him, and a week later he was asked to 4. **at**_____ an 5. **in**_____. He was 6. **of**_____ the job that same day.

As he lived in a small town outside the city, he had to 7. **co**_____ every day. He was a 8. **hi**_____ and so very soon was 9. **pr**_____ to a better position. However, the company he worked for was having problems. Two people were 10. **di**_____ for 11. **em**_____ from the petty cash box, three got the 12. **sa**_____ for continual 13. **ab**_____, two of their friends 14. **re**_____ in sympathy and then most of the workforce 15. **wa**_____ in support. A few weeks later, the directors decided to 16. **la**_____ fifteen 17. **sh**_____ workers because there wasn't enough work, and the managing director decided to 18. **re**_____ early. The atmosphere was so bad that Ian eventually decided to 19. **ha**_____ his 20. **no**_____.

Part 2

In this text, the *first* letter of each word in **bold** is in the *correct* place, but the other letters have been mixed up. Rearrange the letters to make words.

Ian couldn't afford to be 21. **upedmloyen**, however, so he started 22. **jbo hgnnuti** again. A computer company had a 23. **vnyaacc** for position of 24. **smlesana**. A lot of 25. **cidnteadsa** with good 26. **qnafsuliictioa** and 27. **eeerinepcx** applied, and Ian was one of them. After all the interviews had finished, the directors made a 28. **striotlsh** of the best 29. **anpipctlsa**, then invited them back for another interview. After a lot of discussion, they 30. **apndoipet** Ian.

Ian was delighted. After all, he would receive a 31. **slyraa** of £25,000 32. **pre amunn**, with a 5% 33. **iteenmncr** twice a year, a 34. **csnmioiosm** for each computer he managed to sell, excellent 35. **psrke** such as private health insurance and a company car, a company 36. **pnosnie** plan to make sure he would be well-off when he retired, and the chance of 37. **pmotoonir** to the position of sales manager. All in all, his future 38. **psocrsept** looked excellent.

Abbreviations and acronyms

Test your human resources abbreviations. Look at these abbreviations, then complete the crossword puzzle on the next page with the words that are missing from their complete forms. You will find all of these, together with their definitions, in the *Bloomsbury Dictionary of Human Resources and Personnel Management*. The first one has been done for you.

Across

1. VAT = Value Added _____.

2. O and M = organisation and _____.

4. GMP = guaranteed _____ pension.

6. PBR = payment by _____.

9. MD = Managing _____.

11. EOC = _____ Opportunities Commission.

12. INSET = in-service _____.

15. QWL = quality of _____ life.

17. R and D = _____ and development.

20. HR = human _____.

21. SERPS = state earnings-related _____ scheme.

23. In £25K, K means _____.

26. ASAP = as soon as _____.

28. PIW = period of _____ for work.

30. MPP = maternity pay _____.

31. CV = curriculum _____.

33. SWOT analysis = strengths, weaknesses, _____ and threats analysis.

36. LIFO = last in, _____ out.

38. PAYE = pay as you _____.

41. EAT = employment _____ tribunal.

42. MBA = Master of Business _____.

43. PEST = political, economic, social and _____.

Down

1. TOIL = _____ off in lieu.

3. OTE = on-target _____.

5. AGM = annual general _____.

7. ILO = International _____ Organisation.

8. PR = public _____.

10. PLC = _____ limited company.

13. ESOP = employee share _____ plan.

14. TNA = training needs _____.

16. NI = national _____.

18. SAYE = _____ as you earn.

19. EAP = employee _____ programme.

22. TQM = total _____ management.

24. CPD = continuing personal _____.

25. NVQ = National _____ Qualification.

27. PIN = personal _____ number.

29. AVC = additional voluntary _____.

32. PERT = programme _____ and review technique.

34. SMP = statutory _____ pay.

35. CEO = Chief Executive _____.

37. EHO = environmental _____ officer.

39. SSP = statutory _____ pay.

40. p.a. = per _____.

Company positions

Read this text in which someone is describing the different people who work in her company, then match the names of the different people with their positions on the next page. The first one has been done for you.

Welcome to the Bristol division of Compuflop plc. My name is **Marion Smith**, and I am responsible for the company's productive use of its workforce. This is **Alice Ranscombe**, who works in my department typing letters, filing documents, arranging meetings and so on. And this is **Jessica Hopkins**, who does lots of small jobs in and around the office. If you need some filing done, some letters posted, or want a cup of tea, she's the one to ask. The man in the office over there wearing the Versace suit and the Rolex is **Eddie Rolfe**. He controls the company finances. You probably saw his Ferrari parked outside when you arrived. The man over there sweeping the floor is **Reg McEnery**. Reg, when you've finished, could you empty the bins please?

Let me tell you about some of the other people who are currently working in my company. First of all, there's **Anne Kennedy**, who is appointed by the shareholders to help run the company. She spends a lot of time working with **Ronald Anderson**, who makes sure the company is running efficiently, and he has to answer to **Elizabeth Watkins**, who is the most important director in charge of the company. **Susie Farraday** works for Ms Watkins, and she performs various secretarial and administrative duties for her. **Alan Johnson** presides over the company's board meetings, and **Brian Larrs** attends the board meetings only to give advice.

Our company makes computer components, and we need to make sure that production keeps up with demand. **Stephen Bird** is the man who supervises the production process, and he is helped in this job by **Ray Harrison**. In addition to our Bristol office and factory, we also have an office in Birmingham: **Mary Myers** is responsible for the company's work there. **Richard Giddings** is the one who makes sure people know about our products and services. To tell you the truth, I don't think he's doing a very good job; the company doesn't seem to have made much money for quite a long time now.

On the factory floor we have **Harry Rampling**. He's a highly skilled worker, so he's in charge of all the workers on the factory floor. **Andy Kelly** represents the workers in discussions with the managers about things like wages and conditions of employment. At the moment, there is a dispute between the workers and the management about money. The workers want more, and the management say the company can't afford to give a pay rise. Anyway, the company has brought in **Jennie Wilkinson** to help sort things out (she doesn't work for our company and isn't concerned with the dispute, so hopefully she will be able to settle it - the last time we had a dispute, we had to bring in **Jack Langsdale** from the government to make the two sides agree). I do hope the workers don't go on strike again. We've lost a lot of business because of industrial action recently.

© Bloomsbury Publishing Plc. For reference see *Dictionary of Human Resources and Personnel Management* (ISBN 0 7475 6623 2)

We also have a few other people who are here on a temporary basis. **Tabitha Bradley** is one of them. She finished university last month, and she's learning a bit about the company. She's hoping to work with us in the future.

I'm sorry, I didn't catch your name. **Tony Preston**. Nice to meet you Mr Preston. And why are you here? You're here to take over the company and close it down?! Oh dear, I didn't realise we were in that much trouble!

1. Marion Smith	A. area manager
2. Alice Ranscombe	B. official mediator
3. Jessica Hopkins	C. official receiver
4. Eddie Rolfe	D. chief executive officer
5. Reg McEnery	E. foreman
6. Anne Kennedy	F. production manager
7. Ronald Anderson	G. company director
8. Elizabeth Watkins	H. Girl Friday
9. Susie Farraday	I. human resources manager
10. Alan Johnson	J. trade union representative
11. Brian Larrs	K. personal assistant
12. Stephen Bird	L. arbitrator
13. Ray Harrison	M. assistant manager
14. Mary Myers	N. chairman
15. Richard Giddings	O. managing director
16. Harry Rampling	P. graduate trainee
17. Andy Kelly	Q. secretary
18. Jennie Wilkinson	R. non-executive director
19. Jack Langsdale	S. advertising manager
20. Tabitha Bradley	T. caretaker
21. Tony Preston	U. accountant

© Bloomsbury Publishing Plc. For reference see *Dictionary of Human Resources and Personnel Management* (ISBN 0 7475 6623 2)

Complete this job advertisement with appropriate words from the box. The first one has been done for you.

annum • applicant • attractive • basic • benefits • colleagues • commission
covering • CV • drive • experience • increment • ~~leading~~ • motivate
package • post • qualified • rewards • salary • team • vacancy

(1) _Leading_ manufacturing company APB has a (2)_____ for the (3)_____ of

Sales manager

to begin work in our busy Manchester office from this September.

The successful (4)_____ will be suitably (5)_____ and should have had extensive (6)_____ in sales management. They will be able to work as part of a (7)_____, and should have (8) _____ and the ability to (9)_____ and inspire their (10)_____.

In return, we can offer an (11)_____ (12)_____ (13)_____, which includes a (14)_____ (15)_____ of £20K per (16)_____, 10% (17)_____ on all sales, a guaranteed annual (18)_____ of £1K, and other (19)_____ such as a company car and free meals.

If you are interested in working for this us, send your (20)_____ with a (21)_____ letter to:

APB Ltd, Norton Towers, Blackberry Way, Whittersley, WH8 4RT

APB is an equal opportunities employer

© Bloomsbury Publishing Plc. For reference see _Dictionary of Human Resources and Personnel Management_ (ISBN 0 7475 6623 2)

Job description

Complete this job description with words from the box. There are three words that you do not need. The first one has been done for you.

accountability • agree • Benefits • Branch • deal • ensure • Full time • Head Hours • Key • Leave • Location • negotiate • inspect • Part time • produce Reports • responsibilities • Responsible • Shift • supervise • ~~title~~ • visit

Job Description

Job (1) _title_ :   Regional Production manager

(2)_____: Ealing (3)_____, West London

(4)_____ to: Production Manager, (5) _____ Office.

(6) _____   (7)_____. Monday to Friday 9.00 - 5.30

(8) _____ entitlement: 21 days per annum, + bank holidays.

Main (9)_____: To (10)_____ the work of the production department.

(11)_____ (12)_____:

- To (13)_____ product specifications with sales departments and time schedules with stock control department.

- To (14)_____ product is manufactured according to agreed specifications and within time schedules.

- To (15)_____ quality of finished product.

- To (16)_____ sales reports for Head Office.

- To (17)_____ with suppliers on base material prices.

- To (18) _____ suppliers on a regular basis to check quality of base materials.

- To (19)_____ with problems as they rise on a day-to-day basis.

(20)_____ for managing: 1 sub-manager, 10 machinists, 3 trainees, 2 cleaners.

© Bloomsbury Publishing Plc. For reference see *Dictionary of Human Resources and Personnel Management* (ISBN 0 7475 6623 2)

Application forms

Complete this job application form with appropriate words from the box. The first one has been done for you as an example.

> absence • absent • address • approach • assessment • attended • college • contact
> dates • Degree • Diploma • dismissal • duties • education • email • employer
> ~~employment~~ • examinations • false • first name • history • home • illness • information
> leaving • offer • present • postcode • qualifications • reason • referees • suitability
> surname • title • training • university

Application for (1) _employment_ as:	*Telesales Manager*

(2)_____: *Sheppard*   (3)_____(s): *Eric John*

(4)_____: *136 Wrenhouse Street, Endham, Berkshire.*

(5)_____: *RG87 6GH*

(6)_____ details

(7)_____ telephone: *01988 879910*   (8)_____: *ericshep @ freemail.co.uk*

(9)_____ and (10)_____:

Last school (11) _____: *Briarwood Secondary, Endham*

(12)_____ or (13)_____: *North London University, Holloway Road, London.*
                                    Central Business School, Addingsbury

(14)_____ and (15)_____:

A-Levels: Economics, History, Geography
BA (16)_____ in Business Administration (Upper second with Honours)
RSA (17)_____ in Business IT.

Employment (18)_____.

(19)_____ employer and   *Safenet Insurance, Unit 76 Millsfarm Estate, Tottenham, London N17*
(20)_____ of employment: *8YT*
                               2002 - Present.

Job (21)_____: *Assistant telesales manager and coordinator.*

(22)_____: *Cold-calling potential clients for Insurance scheme. Monitoring other telesales operatives as part of quality control.*

(23)_____ for (24)_____: *I would like to develop my potential in sales and marketing, and have more responsibility.*

(25)_____.
Please give the names of two people who can give an (26)_____ of your (27)_____ for this job (one of whom should be your present (28)_____):

1. *Mr Boyd Walton (Manager)*   2. *Alice Waugh (Ex-colleague)*
Safenet Insurance   *Burrett and Dowling Insurance*
(Address above)   *15A Searle Street*
                                       Rigdenbury HB2 9TY

No (29)_____ will be made to your present employer before an (30)_____ of employment is made to you.

If you have had an (31)_____ in the last two years which has caused you (32)_____ from work, please give details with the number of days you were (33)_____.

I confirm that the above (34)_____ is correct to the best of my knowledge. I accept that deliberately providing (35)_____ information could result in my (36)_____.

© Bloomsbury Publishing Plc. For reference see *Dictionary of Human Resources and Personnel Management* (ISBN 0 7475 6623 2)

The recruitment process

This text about the recruitment process below has been divided into three parts. Complete each part with the words and expressions in the boxes. The first answer for each part has been done for you.

<u>Part 1</u>

affirmative recruitment • applicants • appointments • benefits description • disabilities • discrimination • equal opportunities experience • externally • institutional agency • increments internally • job centres • journals • leave • personal qualities private recruitment agency • qualifications • recruitment agency rewards • situations vacant • ~~vacancy~~

When a company or organisation has a 1. _vacancy_ for a new member of staff, it usually advertises the post. It does this 2._____ (for example, in the company magazine or on a company notice board) or 3._____, either in the 4._____ or 5._____ section of a newspaper, in specialist trade 6._____ or through a 7._____ which helps people to find employment. There are two main types of agency. The first of these is the 8._____, usually found in a school or university. These work closely with employers to let potential employees know about the jobs that are on offer (also included in this category are 9._____, which are provided by the state, and which can be found in most main towns in Britain and other countries). The second is the 10._____, which are independent companies, and employers have to pay these agencies for each employee they successfully provide.

A job advertisement has to give an accurate 11._____ of the job and what it requires from the 12._____ (the people who are interested in the post). These requirements might include 13._____ (academic, vocational and professional), work 14._____ in similar lines of work, and certain 15._____ (for example, it might say that you need to be practical, professional and have a sense of humour). The advertisement will also specify what 16._____ (basic salary, commission, regular 17._____, etc) and 18._____ (paid 19._____, free medical insurance, company car, etc) the company can offer in return. The advertisement must be careful it does not break employment laws concerning sex and racial 20._____: some companies emphasise in their job advertisements that they are 21._____ employers (or 22._____ employers in the USA), which means that they will employ people regardless of their sex, skin colour, religion, 23._____, etc.

© Bloomsbury Publishing Plc. For reference see *Dictionary of Human Resources and Personnel Management* (ISBN 0 7475 6623 2)

Part 2

> application • aptitude • board • candidates • covering • ~~CV~~
> group-situational • in-basket • introduction • medical • one-to-one
> pre-selection • psychometric • short-list • turn down

The job advertisement will usually ask people interested in the post to send their 1. _CV_ with a 2._____ letter or a letter of 3._____, or they will ask people to write or call for an 4._____ form. The managers of the company will look at these, and go through a 5._____ procedure, where they choose or 6._____ applicants. They then prepare a 7._____ of possible 8._____: these are the people who will then be invited for an interview. Interviews usually take one of two forms. The first is the 9._____ interview, with one applicant and one employer talking together. The second is the 10._____ interview, with one applicant being interviewed by several people at once.

There may also be tests to see whether the applicant is suitable for the post. There are several of these, including 11._____ tests (which look at psychological traits of the applicant), 12._____ tests, which test the applicant's skills and knowledge, and his / her potential for acquiring more skills and knowledge), 13._____ tests (where several applicants are put into an imaginary situation and decide how to deal with it), and 14._____ tests (in which an applicant has to deal with a number of imaginary tasks similar to those s/he would face in the job). Applicants may also have to go for a 15._____ test to see whether they are healthy enough for the work.

Part 3

> appearance • circumstances • disposition • fixed-term • follow-up
> induction programme • intelligence • interests • offered • open-ended
> potential • probationary • references • ~~seven-point plan~~
> skills • temporary

Many employers use a 1. _seven-point plan_ when they recruit for a new post. They look at different aspects of the applicant to decide whether or not s/he has the correct 2._____ for the job. These include physical 3._____ (for example, is the applicant smart and well-presented?), educational qualifications, general 4._____, special 5._____, hobbies and outside 6._____, mental and emotional 7._____ and family 8._____.

If a candidate gets through the above stages, s/he will be asked to provide 9._____ from people who know him / her, and if these are positive s/he is then 10._____ the post. Before s/he actually starts working, s/he may go through an 11._____ to learn more about the company and the post. Sometimes, s/he may be given a 12._____ contract and have to complete a 13._____ period, where the employers make sure that s/he is suitable for the job before being offered an 14._____ or 15._____ contract. After s/he has been with the company for a while, there might be a 16_____ session, to assess how s/he is getting on in the post.

© Bloomsbury Publishing Plc. For reference see *Dictionary of Human Resources and Personnel Management* (ISBN 0 7475 6623 2)

Personal qualities

At job interviews, candidates are assessed on their suitability for the job they are applying for. In addition to their qualifications and experience, interviewers have to look at the other qualities that make a candidate suitable for a job or not.
The same qualities are also considered when staff receive appraisals and assessments.

Use the nouns and adjectives in the box to complete the sentences. One word can be used twice. The first one has been done for you.

abrasive •	ambition •	conceited •	confidence •	confrontational •	critical
decisive •	impulsive •	industrious •	udgement •	motivation •	obstinate •	~~popular~~
practical •	professional •	punctual •	rapport •	relationship •	reliable •	reserved
	sensible •	sensitive •	selfish •	sociable •	willing	

1. She's very _popular_ : everybody likes her, and enjoys working with her.

2. She isn't very good at making decisions. She's not very _____.

3. He works well with everyone: he has excellent _____ with his colleagues.

4. He always arrives on time. He's very _____.

5. He's always _____ to cover for others when they need to take time off.

6. If you ask her to do something, you know she will do it because she's so _____.

7. She's always pointing out people's faults. She's so _____.

8. He quite _____, and gets upset when people point out his faults.

9. She's very _____ to the needs of others, and will always help people if they have problems.

10. She deals with problems well and makes good decisions, and in that respect she's very _____.

11. He shows excellent _____ when making difficult decisions.

12. She seems to be rather _____ and doesn't mix well with other members of staff.

13. His main problem is that he is extremely _____, and rarely thinks carefully before making important decisions.

14. He's extremely _____, and almost never takes others' advice.

15. He never shares information, and never helps others. I think he's basically _____.

16. She's a very _____ worker, and really enjoys spending time with her colleagues both inside and outside the office.

17. He's very _____ , and always works steadily and hard.

18. He has a very _____ approach; he's clearly well-trained and good at his work, and always does a good job.

19. She's rather _____: she thinks she's much better than everybody else.

20. He clearly has _____, and is keen to move up the company ladder.

21. I think he lacks sufficient _____; he doesn't seem very keen, and always has to be told what to do.

22. She's always arguing with everyone. She has a very poor _____ with her colleagues.

23. One of his main problems is that he lacks _____: he always seems worried and nervous, and always has to check that he's doing the right thing.

24. He has a very _____ manner when you speak to him, and as a result people don't go to him with their problems.

25. People complain that he's very _____, and is always starting arguments or making people angry.

© Bloomsbury Publishing Plc. For reference see *Dictionary of Human Resources and Personnel Management* (ISBN 0 7475 6623 2)

Contract of employment

In this contract there are 31 vocabulary mistakes. Either a word is spelt incorrectly, the form of the word is wrong, or a wrong word has been used. Identify and correct these words. Some of the mistakes occur more than once in the contract.

1.		Term and conditionals of employment
2.	Name of employ:	Avicenna Holdings plc
3.	Name of employed:	Martha Jennings
4.	Job titel:	Personal Assistant to the Managing Director.
5.	Job descriptive:	To perform various secretarial and administrative duty for the MD.
6.	Job locally:	Head Office, Truro.
7.	Celery:	£22,000 per anum (payable monthly in rears)
8.	Started date:	1 April 2005.
9.	Hours of labour:	Full time. 9.15am - 5.45pm Monday until Friday, 1 hour lunch.
10.	Undertime:	Extra hours worked will be paid at the normal hourly rat. Saturdays will be paid at time x 1 ½, Sundays at time x 2.
11.	Holiday enticement:	20 days per anum.
12.	Absent from work:	If for any reason you cannot come to work, you should telephone your manager as soon as possible.
13.	Pension sceme:	The company does not operate a pension sceme. You should arrange this separately.
14.	Dissiplinary and grieving procedures:	Information on these procedures are provided in the staff handybook, together with information on all company police.
15.	Probbation:	All appointments are subjective to three months' probbation, during which time employees may be terminated with two weeks' note on either side.
16.	Terminator:	After successful completion of the probbation period, the note period will be three months.
17.	Referrals:	All apointments are subject to satisfactory referrals.
18.	Singed: *Martha Jennings*	Date: *21 March 2005*

© Bloomsbury Publishing Plc. For reference see *Dictionary of Human Resources and Personnel Management* (ISBN 0 7475 6623 2)

Working hours

Complete the sentences with an appropriate word or expression, and write the answers in the crossword grid on the next page. Clue 1 across has been done for you.

Several of the sentences refer to *shift work* (when employees work for a period and then are replaced by others). Some of the sentences refer to *flexible work systems*, where employees can start or stop work at different hours of the morning or evening, provided that they work a certain number of hours per day or week.

Across (⬇)

1. When somebody is always on time for work, we say that they are _____.

5. When you record the time you leave work by putting a card into a special machine, you _____ _____.

8. A time for which work is paid at twice the normal rate (for example, at weekends or on public holidays) is called _____ *time*.

9. The act of changing an employee's shift or working hours is called *shift* _____.

12. In Britain, parents who have children under 6, or disabled children under 18, have a legal right to have their working hours arranged to help them with their responsibilities. This right is known as *Flexible Work* _____.

13. _____-_____ is the fact of being on time for work (for example, *He was warned for bad* ____-____)

15. _____ *time* is paid time which the management agrees an employee can spend on rest, cleaning or meals, not working.

17. *Time and a* _____ is the normal rate of pay plus 50% extra (for example, when an employee does overtime or works evenings).

18. The _____ *shift* is an informal expression for the night shift.

19. *Shift* _____ are payments made to an employee in addition to their basic pay to compensate them for the inconvenience of the pattern of shift work.

21. A *duty* _____ is a list of times showing when each employee is on duty at those times.

24. _____ is a person's right to something (for example, for a paid holiday, for a minimum of 30 minutes for lunch, for paid sick leave, etc)

25. Hours worked more than the normal working hours are called _____.

26. If a company does not operate a flexible time system, we say that the employees work _____ hours.

27. _____ shifts refers to a system where employees take turns in working different shifts.

Down (➡)

2. The _____ *shift* is another name for the evening shift, just before it gets dark.

3. _____-_____ is a form of employment in which two or more people share a single job, each person working part-time.

4. _____ is a working method where employees work at home on computer terminals, and send the finished material back to the office by email.

6. Employees who work _____-*time* work for the normal working time (i.e. about 8 hours a day 5 days a week).

© Bloomsbury Publishing Plc. For reference see *Dictionary of Human Resources and Personnel Management* (ISBN 0 7475 6623 2)

7. Employees who work _____-*time* do not work for the whole working week (for example, they might only work 4 hours a day instead of 8)

10. A company or organisation that puts a lot of emphasis on flexibility in its employment practices is known informally as a _____.

11. An employee who works _____ *hours* works at times such as in the evening, at night or during public holidays when most people are not at work.

14. _____ *time* is a period when employees working under a flexible time system must be present at work.

16. A company of organisation that puts too little emphasis on flexibility in its working practices is known informally as a _____.

20. _____ is a short form of the expression *flexible time*.

22. A *time* _____ is a record of when employees arrive at and leave work, or one which shows how much time an employee spends on different jobs each day.

23. When an employee is moved systematically from one job to another, this is known as *job* _____.

© Bloomsbury Publishing Plc. For reference see *Dictionary of Human Resources and Personnel Management* (ISBN 0 7475 6623 2)

Appraisals

Look at this list of common appraisal questions. Each one has a word in **bold** in which the letters have been mixed up. Rearrange the letters to make words. The first letter of each word has been underlined. There is an example at the beginning.

1. Do you think the work you are doing meets or exceeds the correct **da̱stnadsr**?
    = *standards*

2. How far do you think you have the skills and **ne̱gdḵwloe** to achieve your duties?

3. How would you describe the **u̱q̱aylit** of the work you are doing?

4. Do you feel you have met the work **bo̱cjetesiv** that were set for you?

5. Do you think you have room for **p̱imoetrenvm**?

6. In your opinion, what are your main **ne̱strsgth** and **se̱sw̱enasek**?

7. Would you benefit from going on a **ṉtrgniai** course?

8. Do you feel you are able to manage your work **hu̱sceled**?

9. Are you happy with your career **o̱grp̱oresnsi** at the moment?

10. Would you like to do something a bit more **egi̱clhglnna**?

11. Are you given help and **me̱e̱oncntgurae** when you need it?

12. What do you like most and what do you like **steaḻ** about the job you are doing?

13. How do you feel about your **odkaorḻw̱**?

14. Is your current job **sc̱ḏeonritip** accurate?

15. Are your job duties clearly **ede̱nḏfi**?

16. Do you feel that there are enough opportunities for **madṯanceven**?

17. Do you have any suggestions for **iṉiprmgvo** your current job?

18. Are you happy with the **ae̱mrlo** in your department?

19. What are your working **shiṟeltoipsan** like with your colleagues?

20. Do you feel **ḏiceslipin** is fair in your department?

21. Does your manager show you fair **e̱tetatrnm** at all times?

22. Does your manager deal **trypop̱ml** with problems?

23. Does your manager deal efficiently with staff **pa̱contmlis**?

24. Does your manager inform you of your **grop̱esrs**?

25. Does your manager give **rep̱isa** for work well done?

26. How do you feel about the **f̱litaisiec** and services provided (for example, office accommodation, security, HR services, etc)?

27. Do you feel that the health and safety **p̱onsrvisoi** are adequate?

28. How do you feel about the pay and **ntḇesefi** you are receiving?

29. Would you **me̱rmdecon** this company as an employer to others?

30. Have you got any other **mo̱cstemn** you would like to make?

© Bloomsbury Publishing Plc. For reference see *Dictionary of Human Resources and Personnel Management* (ISBN 0 7475 6623 2)

Rewards and benefits 1

Exercise 1

Complete these sentences with words which you will find hidden in the box on the next page. The words can be found by reading to the right (▶) and down (▼). The first one has been done as an example.

1.   Extra money paid to employees in dangerous jobs is called _danger_ money.

2.   When we remove money from somebody's wages (for example, because they are late), we say that we _____ their wages.

3.   When we work for more than the normal working time, we say that we work _____.

4.   Time for which work is paid at twice the normal rate (for example, at weekends or on public holidays) is called _____ time.

5.   Money that is removed from our wages to pay for tax and national insurance is called a _____.

6.   _____ refers to the wages employees receive _before_ tax, insurance, etc have been removed. _____ refers to the wages _after_ tax, insurance, etc, has been removed.

7.   An automatic and regular increase in pay is called an _____.

8.   The _____ wage is the lowest hourly wage which a company can legally pay its employees.

9.   A wage is money that is normally paid to an employee on a weekly basis, and a _____ is money that is normally paid to an employee monthly on a regular basis.

10. When the money that an employee receives rises automatically by the percentage increase in the cost of living, we say that it is _____-linked.

11. When British employees want more money for the work they do, they ask for a _rise_. When North American employees want more money, they ask for a _____.

12. A _____ plan is a plan to help people save money for when they retire from work.

13. When an employee wants some of his / her wages paid in advance, s/he might ask his / her manager for a _____.

14. An extra payment in addition to a normal payment is called a _____.

15. A _____ shows an employee how much pay s/he has received, and how much has been removed for tax, insurance, etc.

16. A _____ is the list of people employed and paid by a company.

17. When an employer pays an employee his/her wages directly into his / her bank account, we say that it is paid by direct _____.

18. A pay _____ is the money and other benefits offered with a job.

© Bloomsbury Publishing Plc. For reference see _Dictionary of Human Resources and Personnel Management_ (ISBN 0 7475 6623 2)

19.   Wages are normally paid in _____, which means that they are paid at the end of the working period (for example, at the end of the week or month that the employee has worked).

20.   A _____ is an additional amount of money paid to an employee to compensate him / her for living in an expensive area.

21.   _____ is another word for the money that people receive for working.

p	p	a	d	a	n	g	e	r	a	b	g	m	i	c	w
a	a	r	o	v	e	r	t	i	m	e	r	i	n	b	e
y	y	r	c	d	e	d	u	c	t	i	o	n	c	o	i
r	s	e	k	o	s	u	b	p	e	n	s	i	o	n	g
o	l	a	n	u	d	e	f	g	r	h	s	m	m	u	h
l	i	r	e	b	p	a	c	k	a	g	e	u	e	s	t
l	p	s	t	l	i	j	k	l	i	m	n	m	o	p	i
i	n	c	r	e	m	e	n	t	s	a	l	a	r	y	n
i	n	d	e	x	q	r	s	d	e	p	o	s	i	t	g

Exercise 2

How much can you remember? Without looking back at Exercise 1, complete these sentences with an appropriate word.

1.   If you come late again, we will have to _____ £20 from your wages.

2.   My salary is £2500 _____ a month, but after tax and National Insurance _____, I receive £1850.

3.   The work is challenging and the hours are long, but the company is offering a very attractive pay _____.

4.   Because the company has performed so well this year, the management is delighted to offer a generous end-of-year _____ to all our employees.

5.   We pay £15 an hour, but you get _____ time for working at the weekend and on public holidays.

6.   I think there's been a mistake on my _____: it says I've received £850 this month, but I only got £750.

7.   We don't give you a paycheque: your money is paid to you by direct _____.

8.   There are currently 137 people on the company's _____.

9.   Each year you will automatically receive a pay _____ which is _____-linked to rises in the cost of living.

10.   Wages are usually paid in _____ at the end of each month, but if you need some money before then, we can give you a _____.

© Bloomsbury Publishing Plc. For reference see *Dictionary of Human Resources and Personnel Management* (ISBN 0 7475 6623 2)

Rewards and benefits 2

Exercise 1

Complete the text with appropriate words and expressions from the box. The first one has been done for you.

acceptance bonus • attendance bonus • basic • benefits • commissions • comradeship development • direct • duvet days • extras • extrinsic • fixed flexible • gainsharing • growth • incentive • indirect • insurance • intrinsic motivation • pensions • performance-related • premium bonus • production bonus profit sharing • recognition • satisfaction • security • share • skill • status

Rewards for work fall into two main groups.

The first, and in many opinions the most important, is that of **1.** _direct_ or **2.** _____ rewards. These are real, material rewards, and include **3.** _____ pay (a guaranteed wage or salary paid by the hour, or on a weekly or monthly basis), and **4.** _____ pay, which is linked to how well an employee or a group of employees works. This includes **5.** _____ – money paid to a salesperson or group of salespeople which is usually a percentage of the sales made. Some companies also offer **6.** _____ pay, usually given only to individual employees who work particularly well, or who make a significant contribution to the company. **7.** _____, which is similar to this, is extra money paid to a group or company for increased productivity, and is often offered in order to increase **8.** _____: it is also sometimes known as a **9.** _____. If an employee takes less than the standard time to finish a task, s/he might receive a **10.** _____. Some employers also offer an **11.** _____ for employees who are very rarely absent from work. If an employer is particularly keen to recruit somebody, they might offer him / her an **12.** _____ when s/he agrees to join the organisation. **13.** _____, the practice of dividing profits among the employees, is another reward which is often offered.

In addition to payment, other rewards may be offered. These include **14.** _____ (known informally as **15.** _____) such as a company car, **16.** _____, free meals, **17.** _____ option schemes, holidays, health **18.** _____ and **19.** _____ (a new concept, especially common in the USA, in which an employee can call their office and say they do not feel like coming to work even though they are not ill). Benefits are usually **20.** _____, which means that the employee is not able to choose what s/he gets, but some companies offer **21.** _____ benefits, where the employee can choose from a menu of benefits on offer. **22.** _____ plans, which offer employees increased rewards and benefits for good attendance, behaviour and productivity are becoming increasingly common.

The second group of rewards are **23.** _____ or **24.** _____. These are non-material, and include **25.** _____ (people enjoy being in an important position or a position of authority), job **26.** _____, the opportunities for personal **27.** _____, the chance to learn a new **28.** _____, and career **29.** _____ opportunities. Safety and **30.** _____ at work can also be included in this group, and for most employees, **31.** _____ (being with a group of people you like and get on with) is also a very important reward.

© Bloomsbury Publishing Plc. For reference see *Dictionary of Human Resources and Personnel Management* (ISBN 0 7475 6623 2)

Exercise 2

How much can you remember? Without looking back at the text, answer these questions.

1.   What is the name we give to real material rewards?

2.   What is the name we give to non-material rewards?

3.   Complete this sentence: When pay is linked to how well an employee or a group of employees works, it is called _____ pay.

4.   True or false?: Gainsharing is money paid to somebody when they agree to join a company or organisation.

5.   What might an employee receive if s/he is very rarely absent from work?

6.   What is the informal word for benefits?

7.   Choose the correct option: A benefit in which an employee is allowed to telephone the office to say that s/he does not feel like coming to work is known as a:

(a) **blanket day**   (b) **pillow day**   (c) **quilt day**   (d) **duvet day**   (e) **bedsheet day**

8.   True or false?: benefits that employees can choose from a 'menu' are called flexible benefits.

9.   Choose the correct option: Plans which offer employees increased rewards and benefits for good attendance, behaviour and productivity, etc, are known as:

(a) **inventive plans**   (b) **inedible plans**   (c) **incentive plans**   (d) **inflexible plans**
(e) **indentured plans**

10. Which of these words is closest in meaning to importance and position in society?:

(a) **status**   (b) **statute**   (c) **static**   (d) **statue**   (e) **stateliness**

© Bloomsbury Publishing Plc. For reference see *Dictionary of Human Resources and Personnel Management* (ISBN 0 7475 6623 2)

Holidays and other time off work

Complete these sentences with an appropriate word or words, and write these words in the grid on the next page. If you do this correctly, you will reveal a hidden expression in the shaded vertical strip which means *time off work granted to an employee to deal with personal or family problems*. Some of the letters have already been put into the grid to help you.

Several of the sentences use the word *leave*. In these cases, *leave* is a noun for *permission to be away from work* (e.g. *He isn't here, he's on leave*). Employees can *be* or *go on leave*.

1. A certificate from a doctor to show that an employee has been ill is called a _____ *certificate*.

2. A holiday from work which is fixed by law is called a _____ *holiday*.

3. A period when a woman is away from work to have a baby (but is still paid) is called _____ *leave*.

4. Leave during which an employee receives no money is called _____ *leave*.

5. A period of leave during which an employee is not allowed into the company offices is known informally as _____ *leave*.

6. A period of paid or unpaid time off work for the purposes of research, study or travel is called a _____.

7. The percentage of a workforce which is away from work with no good excuse is called the _____ *rate*.

8. A day when all employees in the country are allowed to take a day off work is called a _____ _____.

9. A period of paid leave given by some companies to staff who have completed several years of service is called _____-_____ *leave*.

10. A person's right to something (for example, their right to a paid holiday from work) is called an _____.

11. If an employee is away from work without permission and without a good reason, we can say that s/he has taken _____ *absence from work*.

12. When an employee is sick and has to wait three days before s/he can claim sick pay, these days are known as _____ *days*.

13. If an employee has permission to be away from work, s/he has leave of _____.

14. When an employee gets time off from work instead of pay (for example, if they work overtime and get some time off work instead of overtime pay), we say that they take *time off* _____ _____.

15. A short period of leave given to a father to be away from work when his partner has a baby is called _____ *leave*.

16. Paid time off from work given to an employee to help him / her deal with personal affairs is called _____ *leave*.

17. A holiday or period when people are not working is called a _____ (especially in the USA).

18. A payment made by the government or by a private insurance company to someone who is ill and cannot work is called *sickness* _____.

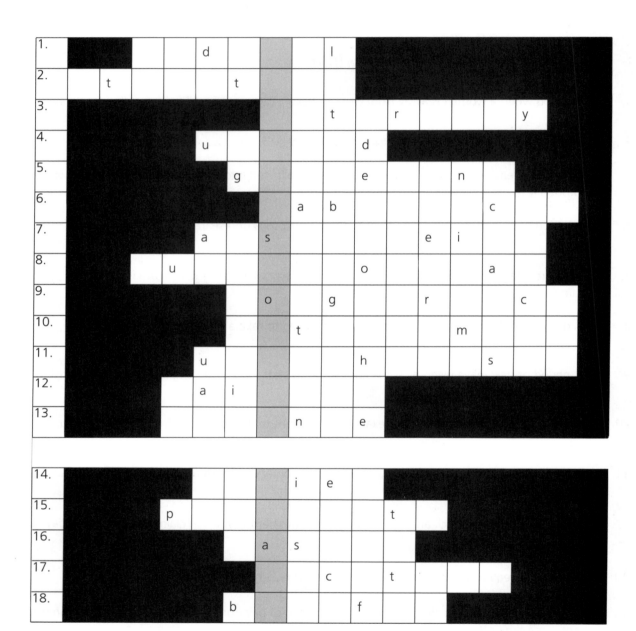

© Bloomsbury Publishing Plc. For reference see *Dictionary of Human Resources and Personnel Management* (ISBN 0 7475 6623 2)

On the next two pages you will see sentences from seven different types of letter. Look at each sentence carefully, then match it with one of the letter types from the list in the box. Underline the key words or phrases which helped you to decide. Be careful - there is one sentence which does not match any of the letter types.

When you have done this, make a list of the useful words and expressions that can be used in these different types of letter.

(A) Invitation to interview   (B) Letter of reference   (C) Letter of appointment
(D) Written warning   (E) Letter of dismissal   (F) Letter of resignation
(G) Acknowledgement of resignation

---

1. I have known Jan Kelly since she started working with the company in 1999.

2. Following the disciplinary interview which you attended on 12 June, I am writing to confirm the decision taken that you will be given a written reprimand under our Disciplinary Procedure.

3. On 7 May, following persistent neglect of duties on your part, you were given a written warning in accordance with the Company's Disciplinary Procedure.

4. She came to work for this company as a Trainee in the production department, and rapidly moved up the scale to become Deputy Production Manager three years ago.

5. Following your interview and our conversation yesterday, this letter is to confirm your post as Production Manager commencing 2 October.

6. This will be placed in your personal record file, but will be disregarded for disciplinary purposes after a period of six months, provided your conduct reaches a satisfactory level.

7. Thank you for your application for the post of Production Manager at Graffix plc.

8. This letter and the attached terms and conditions form the basis of your contract of employment.

9. She is a very able manager, and is particularly keen on keeping up to date with new technology.

10. As I told you yesterday, I have decided to hand in my notice and this letter is to inform you of my decision to leave the company.

11. She has always worked well with other members of staff, has always been on time and has rarely missed work through illness.

12. I am delighted that you will be coming to work for us.

13. The nature of the unsatisfactory conduct was your continual lateness, persistent absenteeism, and neglect of duties on the shop floor.

14. We expect to see an improvement in your punctuality and attendance, and a more professional approach to your work by 30 June.

© Bloomsbury Publishing Plc. For reference see *Dictionary of Human Resources and Personnel Management* (ISBN 0 7475 6623 2)

15. In a letter of 18 June, you were advised that unless your conduct improved, you would be dismissed from your post.

16. We would like you to come for a preliminary interview with our Production Director, James Mills.

17. The notice period indicated in my contract of employment is six weeks, but you agreed during our conversation that in my case this could be reduced to five so as to enable me to take up the offer of another position.

18. Thank you for your letter of 19 October telling us of your intention to leave the company.

19. At the disciplinary hearing held on 16 October, it was decided that your performance was still unsatisfactory, and you had shown no inclination to improve.

20. We are naturally most sorry that you should be leaving us, but I understand your reasons for doing so.

21. I am sure you will find a very pleasant working environment here, and we look forward to welcoming you as a member of our team on 2 October.

22. I am therefore writing to confirm the decision that you will be dismissed, and that your last day of service with the company will be 2 November.

23. These will be held at our Banbury office on 29 and 30 August, and should last about 30 minutes.

24. I would be grateful if you could call me to arrange a suitable time on one of those days.

25. We will be sorry to see her leave, but I know that she is looking for a more challenging position.

26. Unfortunately, I am sorry to tell you that on this occasion your application has been unsuccessful.

27. The likely consequence of insufficient improvement is dismissal.

28. The company you are joining has an excellent reputation, and I am sure you will be as happy there as you have been with us.

29. You have the right to appeal against this decision to the Production Director within seven days of receiving this letter of dismissal, in writing, giving your reasons.

30. As I explained to you, I have been very happy working here, and shall be leaving with many regrets.

31. I have however been offered a post at a substantially higher salary with another company.

32. If you have any special needs, especially concerning access, please let me know in advance.

33. I have noted that your last day of service with us will be 23 November, and I have passed this information to the HR Department to deal with.

34. On a personal level, I shall be particularly sorry to see you go; you have been an excellent manager, and I hope you will keep in touch.

35. In the meantime, if you have any queries about your new post, please do not hesitate to call me on extension 2340.

36. Furthermore, as the prospects of further advancement are greater, I felt that this was an offer I felt I simply could not turn down.

© Bloomsbury Publishing Plc. For reference see *Dictionary of Human Resources and Personnel Management* (ISBN 0 7475 6623 2)

Industrial relations

Industrial relations means the relations between employees and management in an organisation.

Look at these questions, and choose the correct answer for each one.

1. What is the name of an employees' organisation which represents its members in discussions with employers about wages and conditions of employment?

   (a) **a job union**   (b) **an occupation union**   (c) a **vocation union**   (d) **a work union**   (e) **a trade union**

2. What do we call a company which you can only join if you are a member of a particular trade union?

   (a) **a limited shop**   (b) **a full shop**   (c) **a closed shop**   (d) **a barred shop**   (e) **a sweat shop**

3. Unions sometimes put pressure on management to keep their members in their jobs or employ more workers, even if the organisation doesn't need them any more. What is the name of this practice?

   (a) **feather weighting**   (b) **feather fanning**   (c) **feather braining**   (d) **feather bedding** (e) **feather dusting**

4. What is the name of an elected union official who represents employees in day-to-day negotiations with the management?

   (a) **a shop steward**   (b) **a store steward**   (c) **a factory steward**   (c) a **workers' steward** (d) **a department steward**

5. Complete this sentence: Ordinary members of a union or organisation are known as _____ members.

   (a) **safe and sound**   (b) **rank and file**   (c) **cloak and dagger**   (d) **collar and tie** (e) **moan and groan**

6. A union may stop workers from doing certain jobs, especially if they are not a member of that union. This is known as:

   (a) **restrictive practices**   (b) **recumbent practices**   (c) **reductive practices**   (c) **reactionary practices**   (d) **reality practices**

7. Negotiations between employers and workers' representatives over wage increases and conditions is called:

   (a) **collective bargaining**   (b) **correctional bargaining**   (c) **connected bargaining** (d) **corruptive bargaining**   (e) **collapsing bargaining**

8. If workers are unhappy with the way management is treating them, they may work strictly according to the rules of the company as a protest (with the result that production is slowed down). What do we call this method of protest?

   (a) **rule with a rod of iron**   (b) **work-to-rule**   (c) **ruling the roost**   (d) **ruling in favour** (e) **work-by-rules**

9. Workers sometimes try to achieve their demands by not going to work and claiming that they are ill. What is the name of this form of protest?

   (a) **a sickie**   (b) **a sick note**   (c) **a sickout**   (d) **sick leave**   (e) **a sickbag**

© Bloomsbury Publishing Plc. For reference see *Dictionary of Human Resources and Personnel Management* (ISBN 0 7475 6623 2)

10. When workers are unhappy with the management, they sometimes stop working and leave the company building as a protest. What is this action called?

    (a) **a run-out**　(b) **a skip-out**　(c) **a hop-out**　(d) **a jump-out**　(e) **a walk-out**

11. In order to make their workers agree to their conditions, the management of a company may prevent the workers from entering the building. What is this called?

    (a) **a kickout**　(b) **a pushout**　(c) **a blockout**　(d) **a lockout**　(e) **a knockout**

12. When there is a dispute between workers and management, a person who is not concerned with the dispute might be chosen by both sides to try to settle the dispute. What is this person called?

    (a) **an arboretum**　(b) **an archbishop**　(c) **an arbitrator**　(d) **an archer**　(e) **an arraignment**

The next questions use the word *strike* (the stopping of work by workers, usually because of lack of agreement with management, or because of orders from a union).

13. Four of these expressions are *correct*, and one of them is *wrong*. Which one is *wrong*?

    (a) **to strike**　(b) **to go on strike**　(c) **to be on strike**　(d) t**o get on strike**　(e) **to take strike action**

14. What do we call a strike organised suddenly by the workers without the approval of the main union office?

    (a) **a wilddog strike**　(b) **a wildpig strike**　(c) **a wildfire strike**　(d) **a wildflower strike**　(e) **a wildcat strike**

15. Workers usually vote before a strike, to decide if a strike should be held. What is this called?

    (a) **a strike vote**　(b) **a strike ballot**　(c) **a strike election**　(d) **a strike canvass**　(e) **a strike poll**

16. What is the name for a worker who is on strike and standing at the entrance of a place of work to try to persuade other employees not to work?

    (a) **a wicket**　(b) **a cricket**　(c) **a ticket**　(d) **a picket**　(e) **a ricket**

17. What do we call an employee who continues working when a company is on strike?

    (a) **a blackberry**　(b) **a blackhead**　(c) **a blackbird**　(d) **a blackleg**　(e) **a blacksmith**

18. What do we call a strike when all the workers in a country go on strike?

    (a) **a complete strike**　(b) **a formal strike**　(c) **a general strike**　(d) **a country strike**　(e) **a home strike**

Health, safety and welfare

A. Choose the correct words from the box to complete these sentences. Each word comes after *safety*.

> audit • committee • feature • irregularities • egislation • offence
> officer • precautions • regulations • representative

1. Behaviour at work which can cause a hazard is called is safety _____.

2. Actions to try to make sure something is safe at work are called safety _____.

3. An official who checks places of work and work methods to make sure they are safe is called a safety _____.

4. A check of the workplace to see how safety regulations are being implemented is called a safety _____.

5. A group of people set up to examine the health and safety policy of a particular company is called a safety _____.

6. When a place of work is not safe for its employees, customers and contractors (usually because the management have not made sure it is safe, or have not followed safety rules), we say that it has safety _____.

7. Rules that make a place of business safe for employees, customers and contractors are called safety _____.

8. A union member who checks that a company and its methods are safe is called a safety _____.

9. A government law to make sure that places of work are safe is called safety _____.

10. Something on a tool or machine which prevents it from injuring the person using it is called a safety _____.

B. Match the words in the first box with the words in the second box to make safety features that you should find in a place of work.

> emergency • fire • first aid • assembly • smoke

> access • alarm • blanket • bucket • detector • door • escape
> exit • extinguisher • hose • kit / box • officer • point • post

C. Answer these questions about health, safety and welfare.

1. Many employees experience tension or worry at work as a result of overwork, problems with managers, etc. What do we call this?

   (a) **strain**   (b) **struggle**   (c) **strife**   (d) **stress**

2. *RSI* is a pain in the arm or other part of the body felt by somebody who does the same movement many times as part of their job (for example, when keyboarding). What does RSI stand for?

   (a) **regular stress incident**   (b) **repeated self intolerance**   (c) **repetitive strain injury**
   (d) **repressive sickness ignorance**

3. A lot of office equipment (for example, chairs, keyboards, etc) is designed to be more comfortable to use and so helps to prevent RSI. What is the adjective we use to describe objects like this?

   (a) **ergonomic**   (b) **erroneous**   (c) **eponymous**   (c) **equivocal**

4. In some places of work, employees are often ill because of problems in the building itself (for example, blocked air-conditioning ducts, poor lighting, poor ventilation, etc) . What is the name of this problem?

   (a) **ill workplace phenomena**   (b) **sick building syndrome**   (c) **unwell office experience**
   (d) **ailing industrial angst**

5. Before a company has to do a dangerous job, it needs to consider how dangerous the job is, and what precautions it can take. What is this called?

   (a) **danger analysis**   (b) **risk assessment**   (c) **hazard perception**   (d) **troubleshooting**

6. Safety officers inspect some places of work to make sure that they are safe, but in most cases companies have to make sure that health and safety procedures are being followed in the workplace. What is this called?

   (a) **self-control**   (b) **self-satisfaction**   (c) **self-assessment**   (d) **self-regulation**

7. Employees have to follow company instructions on how to behave in the workplace, especially when they are working with dangerous equipment or substances. What are these rules called?

   (a) **rules of the house**   (b) **codes of practice**   (c) **regulations of behaviour**
   (d) **laws of the land**

8. To some extent, a company is responsible for how its employees behave, and the risks they take, while they are at work. What is this called?

   (a) **vicarious liability**   (b) **risk liability**   (c) **limited liability**   (d) **behaviour liability**

9. What do we call an accident which takes place at work?

   (a) **on-the-job accident**   (b) **occupational accident**   (c) **working accident**
   (d) **environmental accident**

10. A safety officer might decide that a workplace is too dangerous, and orders everyone to stop working. What is the name of this order?

    (a) a **cancellation notice**   (b) **a closure notice**   (c) **a prohibition notice**   (d) **a barring notice**

64

Discipline and problems at work

Disciplinary action (action to control or punish bad behaviour by employees) sometimes has to be taken at work. How much do you know about discipline in the workplace? Answer these questions.

A. Rearrange the jumbled letters in **bold** to make words and expressions that describe problems at work that may require disciplinary action. The first letter of each word has been underlined.

1. poor **kiegimpe̱ten**	2. persistent **m̱aisseteben**	3. **nu̱midctocs**
4. **cegelie̱ngn** of duties	5. **eḇhcar** of **tafy̱se** regulations	6. **glip̱snee** on the job
7. **ceisedioednb** (failure to obey instructions)	8. **afdur** (making money by making people believe something that is not true)	9. **hfe̱tt** of money or work equipment
10. **mins̱gok** and / or **griṉdink** on the job or on company premises	11. **ane̱dlig** or using **grus̱d**	12. **lulḇigyn** of colleagues
13. **oni̱tindiatim** of colleagues or customers	14. **enile̱vco** towards colleagues or customers	15. **aa̱rilc sua̱eb** of colleagues or customers
	16. **aes̱ulx maas̱hrenst** of colleagues or customers	17. intentional **gma̱dae** of property or equipment

B. Complete these mini-dialogues with words or expressions from the box.

> aggrieved • alienation • allegation • appeal • disciplinary action • disciplinary board
> dock • down tools • grievance • grievance procedure • hostile work environment
> instant dismissal • insubordination • job dissatisfaction • letter of dismissal
> sackable offence • sexual discrimination • suspend • ultimatum • unfair dismissal
> verbal warning • walk-out

1. A. Sorry I'm late again, Mrs Johnson.
    B. So am I Robert. If you do it again, I'm afraid we'll have to _____ your wages.

2. A. I'm not at all happy with the way the management treat us.
    B. If you have a _____, you should talk to the shop steward.

3. A. There have been complaints of bullying and intimidation on the shop floor.
    B. So I've heard. The workers are all complaining that this is a very _____.

4. A. That's the third time this week that he's been caught smoking in the office.
    B. Well, we should give him an _____: if he does it again, he's out.

5. A. You know you shouldn't use the computers for sending personal emails. I've already given you two _____. The next time, you'll get one in writing.
    B. I'm sorry, it won't happen again.

6. A. What are your views on racial harassment in the workplace?
    B. In my view, it is a _____; anybody who is found guilty of this should be dismissed immediately.

7. A. What's that you've got, Rob?
    B. It's a _____. Apparently the management are very unhappy about my poor timekeeping and have told me to leave.

8. A. I don't believe I've been dismissed for taking too many coffee breaks!
    B. If you think the decision is too harsh, you can _____ and claim _____.

9. A. What happened when you told the foreman he was stupid and incompetent?
    B. I was given a financial penalty for _____.

10. A. The manager said he would only promote me if I paid him some money.
    B. That's a very serious _____. Do you have any proof?

11. A. How do our factory staff feel about the increased working hours and reduced salaries?
    B. Well, naturally, they're very _____. They're threatening to _____ and stage a _____.

12. A. It's not fair. I've got better qualifications and more experience than Brian, but he was awarded the promotion. Just because I'm a woman!
    B. That's terrible. It's always happening here. You should complain about the _____ in this company.

13. A. I'm not the one who's been damaging the machinery. It must be someone else.
    B. I know, Alice. But until we find the person who's been doing it, I'm afraid we have to _____ you for a few weeks.

14. A. What's the _____ in this company?
    B. If you are unhappy with any aspect of your job, talk first of all to your first-line supervisor. He should go to the main supervisor who will take it up with the HR Manager or Department Manager.

15. A. Are you happy here in this company?
    B. Not really. I have a lot of _____. The work is boring, the money is poor and nobody seems to appreciate what I do.

16. A. What happens here if somebody breaks the rules?
    B. If it's serious, they have to appear before a _____ of three senior members of staff, and they decide what _____ to take.

17. A. The work here is boring, the money is terrible, we never seem to see any results and the management never talk to us or ask us for our opinion.
    B. I agree. There's a very strong feeling of _____ here.

18. A. I heard one of our shop assistants being very rude to a customer this morning.
    B. Rudeness is grounds for _____: he'll have to leave immediately.

© Bloomsbury Publishing Plc. For reference see *Dictionary of Human Resources and Personnel Management* (ISBN 0 7475 6623 2)

Personnel training and development

Look at these texts, and decide what each person is talking about. Choose the answers from the box.

action learning • adventure training • assertiveness training • carousel training
continuous personal development • experiential learning
an induction course • in-tray learning • modern apprenticeship • off-the-job training
online learning • open learning • sales training • team-building
total quality management • training needs analysis

1. This company is committed to helping its employees learn about their jobs and develop their skills for the whole period they are working here, and not just at the beginning of their contract. We run regular courses and workshops in order to achieve this, both inside and outside the company premises.

2. Our employees have to deal with a lot of difficult situations, and they often come in contact with people who can be difficult to work with and do business with. We train them to have more confidence in themselves so that they can deal effectively with any problems and difficulties they encounter.

3. We believe that the best way of learning a skill is through practice. We don't waste time on courses and workshops. We show the employee his duties, give him an outline of how the company operates, and then we just say 'Get on with it, and good luck'. It's a remarkably effective method.

4. It's very important that our employees develop skills in leadership, problem solving, decision-making and interpersonal communication. The best way to achieve this is to get them involved in group games and physically demanding outdoor activities like sailing and climbing. These also help to build team spirit.

5. When we promote somebody to a management position, the first thing we do is to give them a lot of typical management paperwork and tell them to deal with it. We set them a time limit for this, and monitor them carefully to see how they get on. We then review their performance and show them where they went right or wrong.

6. Our company understands how important it is that our employees work well together in order for the company to be effective. Our training sessions are designed to instil co-operation and solidarity in a group of employees who have to work together.

7. It is our company policy to make sure that our employees know how all the jobs in the company work, not just their own. We find the best way of doing this is to move them from job to job and department to department. They meet colleagues who they might not normally meet, and learn about their jobs and how they operate.

8. New employees in our company need to learn about our products and how they work, how the distribution system operates, how to deal with both suppliers and customers and how to handle complaints. They also study trade and retail laws, and are accompanied on their first customer visits by their trainer.

9. I've been interested in photography since I was very young, so when I finished school I started learning how to be a photographer. I spend my week working with a professional, who teaches me about all the different aspects of photography. At the same time, I receive training in areas such as numeracy, problem-solving and interpersonal skills.

10. First of all I was given a tour of the factory and then I was introduced to my colleagues and was given an outline of the company and its products. After that I was guided through the company's code of practice, taken to my department and was shown my duties.

11. My company can't hold training workshops in the office because we don't have enough space, and of course while we are learning, we aren't actually making money, so the company feels it wouldn't be making the best use of its employees. Instead, they send us to a college in the evening where we develop our skills and knowledge.

12. This company believes that personal development and training should be more flexible. As a result, we have developed a system of flexible training courses that a trainee or employee can start at any time, and which does not require a teacher.

13. Once a year we look at the different skills and abilities of our staff, and we decide if they are enough to help the company fulfil its aims and operate effectively. We then develop a series of classes and workshops to help the staff learn more about their job and how they can operate more effectively.

14. This company has a policy that our managers should be committed to maintaining and improving the quality of their work, and also their skills and knowledge. We run courses, classes and workshops on a regular basis, and ensure that they are kept up to date with all the latest developments.

15. We are a very forward-looking company and we use the most up-to-date methods, so of course all our training is delivered over the Internet or through our company intranet. This means that our trainees and employees can learn during their breaks, at home and even when they are on holiday.

16. Our company trains its management staff by giving them a series of problem-solving activities. The managers from our office work together with those from other departments around the country to solve real or imaginary problems, and their findings are then applied to the overall successful running of the company.

© Bloomsbury Publishing Plc. For reference see *Dictionary of Human Resources and Personnel Management* (ISBN 0 7475 6623 2)

Answers

Nouns 1 (page 1)

1. peak   2. session   3. facilities   4. retirement   5. assessment   6. mismanagement   7. experience   8. objective   9. mediation   10. potential   11. predecessor   12. supervision   13. ceiling   14. stipulation   15. interview   16. budget   17. forecast   18. motivation

peak, experience, interview, budget and *forecast* can also be verbs

Nouns 2 (page 2)

The words in the box are:
course   dissatisfaction   escalation   expertise   feedback   friction   misconduct   performance   placement   quality   range   ratification   retainer   technique   temp   weighting

The answers are:
1. quality   2. ratification (from the verb *to ratify*)   3. temp (this can also be a verb: *to temp*)   4. performance   5. range (this can also be a verb: *to range*)   6. expertise   7. dissatisfaction   8. misconduct   9. friction   10. course   11. placement   12. retainer   13. weighting   14. feedback   15. escalation (from the verb *to escalate*)

Verbs 1 (page 3)
1. recruit   2. empower   3. consult   4. object   5. negotiate   6. supervise   7. institute / instigate   8. delegate   9. evaluate   10. review

delegate and *review* can also be nouns
The word in the shaded vertical strip is *reconsider*.

Verbs 2 (page 4)

1. process   2. sponsor   3. research   4. headhunt   5. transfer   6. recommend   7. discipline   8. exploit   9. target   10. tender   11. reward   12. disregard   13. direct   14. terminate   15. encourage

process, sponsor, research, transfer, discipline, target, tender and *reward* are also nouns.

Verbs 3 (pages 5 + 6)

1. violated (we can also say *broken* or *abused*)   2. minimise   3. appointed (we can also say *employed, hired* or *taken on*)   4. validate   5. accusing   6. justifying   7. collaborating   8. claimed   9. fund (this can also be a noun)   10. assume   11. questioning   12. observe   13. erode   14. qualified   15. invited

Adjectives 1 (page 7)

1. formal   2. unfilled   3. self confident   4. professional   5. disciplinary   6. stressful   7. groundless   8. optional   9. slack   10. constructive   11. autonomous   12. unanimous   13. successful   14. enterprising   15. salaried   16. continuous   17. consultative   18. staggered

Adjectives 2 (page 8)

1. impartial   2. capable   3. steady   4. irregular   5. discriminatory   6. eligible   7. casual   8. aggrieved   9. able-bodied   10. punctual   11. minimal   12. affiliated   13. voluntary   14. generous   15. acting

Wordbuilding 1: Adjectives (page 9)

1. continual   2. continuous   3. constructive   4. creative / competitive   5. quantifiable   6. comparative   7. boring / repetitive   8. decisive   9. dependable   10. satisfactory   11. preferential   12. admirable   13. apologetic   14. doubtful   15. hopeful   16. careful   17. careless   18. agreeable   19. active   20. obligatory   21. occupational   22. consultative   23. attractive   24. suitable   25. reliable

Wordbuilding 2: Nouns 1 (pages 10 +11)

1. compensation   2. motivation   3. classifications   4. argument   5. replacement   6. signature   7. agreement   8. promotion   9. application   10. authorisation   11. appointment   12. successor   13. qualification(s)   14. permission   15. attendance   16. satisfaction   17. failure   18. negotiation   19. acceptance   20. intervention   21. dismissal   22. consumer   23. contention   24. insurance   25. improvement   26. enticement

Wordbuilding 3: Nouns 2 (page 12)

1. responsibility   2. confidence   3. ✓   4. incompetence   5. flexibility   6. exemption   7. disability   8. ✓   9. difference   10. convenience   11. sympathy   12. accuracy   13. capabilities   14. intelligence   15. ✓

© Bloomsbury Publishing Plc. For reference see *Dictionary of Human Resources and Personnel Management* (ISBN 0 7475 6623 2)

Wordbuilding 4: Opposites (page 13)

1. Indirect   2. unfair / unjustified   3. Inefficient   4. incompatible   5. inadequate   6. irregular   7. unconditional   8. incapable   9. unofficial / illegal   10. indecisive   11. irrecoverable   12. ineligible   13. dissatisfied   14. inexperienced   15. Ineffective   16. unacceptable   17. incompetent   18. insolvent   19. intangible   20. unauthorised   21. impossible   22. unreasonable

Prepositions (page 14)

1. ...sponsored **by** their companies.   2. ...abroad **on** business.   3. ...redundant **during** the recession.   4. ...background is **in** the electronics...   5. ...will meet ~~to~~ your expenses.   6. ...of complaint **to** the manager.   7. ...other companies **by** offering them...   8. ...threatened **to** dismiss him...   9. ...is **at** the discretion...   10. ...granted ~~with~~ compassionate...   11. ...a degree **in** Business Studies   12. ...ten hours ~~for~~ every day.   13. ...away **on** maternity leave.   14. ...to overcome ~~on~~ several obstacles...   15. ...is equivalent **to** that of...   16. ...have noticed ~~on~~ an improvement...   17. He is **in** full-time employment,   18. ...no grounds **for** dismissal.   19. ...it is also **against** the law.   20. ...the day **after** tomorrow.   21. **Under** the terms of...   22. We rely **on** our suppliers...   23. ...responsible **for** causing...   24. ...can't work **under** pressure,...   25. ...she took ~~out~~ a job...   26. I look forward **to** hearing...

Working words (page 15)

1. with / from / This / on   2. which / one / the   3. ago / used / These / to / or   4. of / manages *or* seems   5. the / where   6. Between / by   7. of / most *or* many / near   8. to / no / of   9. not / even / at *or* over   10. on / be   11. Unless / will / a   12. at / knowing / would / in   13. what / from / was   14. At / more / since *or* as *or* because / had   15. as / anyone *or* anybody *or* everybody   16. who / just   17. with / made   18. from / until / that / off   19. by / had   20. in / to / of / which

Formal words 1 (page 16)

1. analyse (spelt *analyze* in American English)   2. assessed at   3. averted   4. administer   5. assigned   6. annulled   7. audit   8. appealed to   9. addressed   10. award   11. admonished   12. awaiting   13. adjusted   14. adjourned   15. appointed   16. apportioned   17. attend   18. advised   19. assist   20. amalgamated

Formal words 2 (pages 17 + 18)

Across: 2. retain   6. briefed   7. consented   8. sequestered (we can also say *sequestrated*)   12. settle   15. outlined   17. reinstated   18. tender   19. dismissed   20. engage (we can also say *employ* or *hire*)   21. upgraded
Down: 1. waived   3. notified   4. present (note the pronunciation: **/prɪ'zent /**)   5. undertaken   7. consulted   8. specify   9. elected   10. redeployed   11. indexed (this is usually used in passive constructions - *is / are indexed*)   13. inquiring (also spelt *enquiring*)   14. licensed   16. enter

Word association 1 (page 19)

1. cost (usually used in the plural - *cost<u>s</u>* - after *marginal*)   2. minimum   3. salary   4. strike   5. shift   6. medical   7. labour   8. employment   9. insurance   10. income   11. private   12. pension   13. staff   14. contract   15. personal

curriculum vitae should appear in the shaded vertical strip (usually abbreviated to *CV*. A CV is known as a *résumé* in the USA). For more information on CVs, see the note under the answers for 'Job advertising'.

Word association 2 (page 20)

1. work (these verbs can also be followed by *a job*)   2. instructions   3. qualifications   4. redundancy (*announce* is usually followed by the plural *redundancies*; *receive* and *take* are usually followed by *redundancy <u>payment</u>*)   5. a salary (these verbs can also be followed by *a wage* or *wages*)   6. a contract   7. a job (these verbs can also be followed by *work*. Note that *job* is countable and *work* is uncountable: we cannot say *a work*)   8. an appointment   9. a tax (or *taxes*)   10. accounts   11. resignation (these verbs are followed by pronouns such as *your, his, her,* etc)   12. a pension   13. complaint (*be cause for* is not usually followed by an article - *We have no cause for ~~a~~ complaint*)   14. rules   15. a post (not *work* or *a job*, because *fill* or *be appointed to* cannot be used with these words. *Be appointed to* is usually followed by *the* : *He was appointed to <u>the</u> post of senior executive*)

Word association 3 (page 21)

Part 1:
The words in the box are: computer, staff, tax, management, business, self-, labour, pay, career, company, sales, job, industrial
Part 2:
1. pay   2. tax   3. management   4. job   5. labour   6. industrial   7. company   8. sales   9. staff   10. computer   11. career   12. business   13. self-

Word association 4: Expressions with salary and wage (page 22)

1. liveable   living   basic   nominal   minimum   monthly   average   annual   yearly (although annual and yearly would not normally come before *wage*, as *wages* are usually paid weekly, often in cash, and tend to be for manual or short-term work. *Wage* can also be preceded by *daily* and *weekly*)
2. (a) + (b): draw / earn (in either order)   (c) + (d) + (e) + (f) + (g): pay / raise / reduce / cut / offer (in any order)   (h) dock   (i) + (j): fall / rise (in either order)   (k) command

continued on next page

© Bloomsbury Publishing Plc. For reference see *Dictionary of Human Resources and Personnel Management* (ISBN 0 7475 6623 2)

Word association 4: *salary* and *wage* (page 22) *continued*

3. (a) True   (b) False. It is called a *wage formula*   (c) False. Price rises encourage higher wage demands, and these make prices rise even more.   (d) True   (e) False. Wages are not allowed to increase.   (f) False. They are called *wage differentials*. (g) False. It is the lowest legal wage for a particular class of worker.   (h) True

4. (a) deductions   (b) structure   (c) drift (also called *earnings drift*)   (d) expectations   (e) review (also called a *pay review*)   (f) ceiling (we can also say *wage ceiling*)   (g) bands   (h) cut

Word association 5: *work* and *working* (page 23)

A.
work: ethic   experience   flow   load (usually written as one word: *workload*)   measurement   out (a phrasal verb: *to work out* a period of notice)   overload (we also say *overwork*)   rage (an informal expression)   sampling   schedule   shadow   sharing   standard   stoppage   structuring   team
working: conditions   day   hours   lunch (also called a *power lunch*)   practices   supervisor (this is a unisex word which has a similar meaning to *foreman*)   week

B.
1. work overload   2. working conditions   3. work measurement   4. work experience   5. working hours   6. working supervisor   7. work out   8. Work rage   9. working practices   10. work schedule   11. working lunch   12. work stoppages

Two-word expressions 1 (page 24)

Exercise 1:
accession rate   bonus scheme   childcare provision   disciplinary action   employer's liability   freelance worker   grievance procedure   human capital   incentive plan   job satisfaction   know-how   line manager   milk round   needs assessment   occupational mobility   promotion ladder   quality time   replacement rate   shift differential   team spirit   upward communication   voluntary redundancy   wrongful dismissal   yes-man

Exercise 2:
1. disciplinary action   2. voluntary redundancy   3. milk round   4. needs assessment   5. occupational mobility   6. accession rate   7. promotion ladder   8. know-how   9. wrongful dismissal   10. replacement rate

Two-word expressions 2 (page 25)

The following two-word expressions can be found in the two boxes:
adverse action   advisory arbitration   age discrimination   allowed time   ancillary staff   appraisal interview   attendance time   body language   career path   collaborative working   collective bargaining   corporate climate   dress code   earnings drift   fast track   gross negligence   group dynamics   health screening   hot desking   immediate dismissal   incremental scale   ineffective time   information overload   job opportunities   negligent reference   notice period   official dispute   problem solving   racial discrimination   reward package   restrictive covenant   result driven   selection procedure   severance pay   sex discrimination   skills inventory   tertiary sector   track record   value mesh

You can find all of these expressions, together with their definitions and sample sentences, in the *Bloomsbury Dictionary of Human Resources and Personnel Management* (ISBN 0 7475 6623 2)

Phrasal verbs 1 (pages 26 + 27)

Across: 3. closing   5. make   6. get   8. dragged   12. fighting   14. follow   16. went   17. set   18. turned   21. held   22. fallen
Down: 1. handed   2. working   4. weed   7. carried   9. cancelled (spelt *canceled* in American English)   10. fill   11. phased   13. sort   15. opt   19. run   20. back

Phrasal verbs 2 (page 28)

1. held back   2. gearing up for   3. build into   4. standing in for   5. brought up   6. fill in   7. held down   8. burn out   9. gave way to (we can also say *gave in to*)   10. break off   11. get across   12. stand off (compare this with *lay off*, which is used in a different way)

The phrasal verb in the shaded vertical strip is *bring forward*.

Phrasal verbs 3 (page 29)

1. D   2. I   3. M   4. O   5. H   6. A   7. E   8. J   9. L   10. B   11. G   12. N   13. F   14. C   15. K

Phrasal verbs 4 (page 30)

1. ✓   2. ✓   3. get ahead   4. ✓   5. ✓   6. broke down   7. ✓   8. handed over   9. ✓   10. called off   11. give in to   12. phased in   13. ✓   14. took up   15. backed out   16. give up   17. ✓   18. put out   19. ✓   20. ✓

answer key

Idioms 1: The people you work with (page 31)

1. a happy camper (the opposite is an *unhappy camper*)   2. a whizz-kid   3. a toxic employee   4. a seagull manager   5. a spear carrier   6. a workaholic   7. a plug-and-play employee   8. a pilot fish   9. a self-made man   10. a free worker   11. a nethead   12. a mover and shaker   13. a yes-man   14. a moonlighter (the verb is *to moonlight*)   15. a Man Friday (a woman who does the same thing is called a *Girl Friday*. We often say *Person Friday* to avoid sexism)   16. an idea hamster   17. a heavy hitter   18. a boomerang worker   19. an empty suit   20. a goldbricker   21. a digithead   22. a hip shooter

Idioms 2 (page 32)

1. (d)   2. (c)   3. (b)   4. (a)   5. (a) (this is a rather sexist expression, which you should avoid using)   6. (d)   7. (d)   8. (b)   9. (d)   10. (a) (in the USA, it is known as a *gravy job*)   11. (c)   12. (d)

Idioms 3 (page 33)

1. leaky reply   2. shape up or ship out   3. graveyard shift   4. kiss up to   5. dead wood   6. glad-hand (= to shake hands with people)   7. dress-down day   8. ear candy   9. eye service   10. dumbsizing (an idiomatic word derived from *downsizing* - the act of reducing the number of employees in a company. *Dumb* has a similar meaning to *stupid*)   11. sweetener (for example, a salary increase, more perks, etc)   12. helicopter view

Remember that these are *informal* expressions, and you would only use them in informal, spoken situations. You should <u>not</u> use them in formal or semi-formal letters.

Changes (pages 34 + 35)

<u>Exercise 1: Verbs</u>
1. streamline   2. promoted   3. renovated   4. increased (we can also say *risen*)   5. renewed   6. release   7. retire   8. redeployed (this is similar to *transferred*)   9. expanded / increased   10. relax   11. decreased (we can also say *fell* or *dropped*)   12. enforce (we can also say *tighten up*)   13. demoted (we can also say *downgraded*, but this is less common)   14. replace   15. deteriorated   16. adjusted / increased   17. reduce   18. phased in (the opposite is *phased out*)   19. adapt / adjust   20. lay off (the opposite is *take on*, *hire*, *appoint* or *employ*)   21. relocated   22. downgraded   23. downsize   24. alter (we can also say *amend*, *revise* or *modify*)

<u>Exercise 2: Nouns</u>
1. E   2. B   3. A   4. D   5. D   6. A   7. C   8. E   9. F   10. A   11. D   12. E   13. G   14. B   15. A   16. D   17. D   18. E   19. E

Over and under (pages 36 + 37)

1. underworked   2. overrun   3. overmanned / overstaffed   4. overpaid   5. underachiever (the opposite is *overachiever*)   6. understudy (this can also be a verb: *to understudy*)   7. undertaking   8. overqualified   9. overheads (American English is usually *overhead*)   10. overworked (the noun is *overwork*: '*She is suffering from overwork*')   11. undermine   12. overturn   13. overrule   14. underutilised   15. overhaul   16. undertaking   17. overtime (useful expressions with *overtime* include: *overtime ban*; *overtime pay*; *overtime rate*)   18. undermanned   19. overrated   20. understanding

A career case history (page 38)

1. apply   2. filled in (we can also say *filled out*)   3. application form   4. attend   5. interview   6. offered   7. commute   8. high achiever   9. promoted (the opposite is *demoted*)   10. dismissed (we can also say *fired* or *sacked* - these are less formal)   11. embezzlement   12. sack   13. absenteeism   14. resigned   15. walked out   16. lay off   17. shop floor   18. retire (we can also say *take early retirement*)   19. hand in   20. notice   21. unemployed   22. job hunting   23. vacancy   24. salesman (we often use the word *salesperson* to avoid sexism)   25. candidates   26. qualifications   27. experience   28. shortlist   29. applicants (*applicant* and *candidate* are very similar in meaning)   30. appointed (we can also say *hired*)   31. salary (a *salary* is usually paid monthly in the form of a cheque: compare this with *wage*, which is often paid weekly, in cash)   32. per annum   33. increment   34. commission   35. perks   36. pension   37. promotion   38. prospects

Abbreviations and acronyms (pages 39 + 40)

<u>Across:</u> 1. tax   2. methods   4. minimum   6. results   9. Director   11. Equal   12. training   15. working   17. research   20. resources   21. pension   23. thousand   26. possible   28. incapacity   30. period   31. vitae   33. opportunities   36. first   38. earn   41. appeal   42. Administration   43. technical
<u>Down:</u> 1. time   3. earnings   5. meeting   7. Labour   8. relations   10. public   13. ownership   14. analysis   16. insurance   18. save   19. assistance   22. quality   24. development   25. Vocational   27. identification   29. contributions   32. evaluation   34. maternity   35. officer   37. health   39. sick   40. annum (*p.a.* = *per annum*. PA = *personal assistant*)

72

© Bloomsbury Publishing Plc. For reference see *Dictionary of Human Resources and Personnel Management* (ISBN 0 7475 6623 2)

Company positions (pages 41 + 42)

1. I   2. Q   3. H   4. U   5. T   6. G   7. O   8. D   9. K   10. N   11. R   12. F   13. M   14. A   15. S   16. E   17. J   18. L   19. B   20. P   21. C

Recruitment advertising (page 43)

1. leading   2. vacancy   3. post   4. applicant   5. qualified   6. experience   7. team   8. drive   9. motivate   10. colleagues   11. attractive   12. rewards   13. package   14. basic   15. salary   16. annum (*per annum = in a year*)   17. commission   18. increment   19. benefits (also called *perks*)   20. CV* (= *curriculum vitae*. Plural = *curriculums vitae*. A CV is known as a *résumé* in American English)   21. covering (a *covering letter* is a letter sent with other documents to say why you are sending them. It should be brief and to the point. For example, when applying for a job, you should explain that you are interested in the job and that you are *attaching* or *enclosing your CV.*)

*A CV is a summary of your work experience (current and previous places of work, job title, duties, dates) and qualifications (school, university, college; academic, professional and vocational). It should also include your contact details (address, telephone number, email, etc). You could also include your date of birth, your hobbies and interests (if you think these might be relevant or useful) and current salary. Some people also include their references on their CV. A CV should be *updated* on a regular basis.

Job description (page 44)

1. title   2. Location   3. Branch   4. Reports   5. Head   6. Hours   7. Full time   8. Leave (we can also say *Holiday*)   9. accountability (*Main accountability* is also called *Summary of position* or *Job purpose summary*)   10. supervise (we can also say *oversee)*   11. Key   12. responsibilities (*Key responsibilities* are also called *Main activities*)   13. agree   14. ensure   15. inspect   16. produce   17. negotiate   18. visit   19. deal   20. Responsible

Many unions insist on clear *demarcation* for their members: this is a clear definition of the responsibilities of each employee in a company.

Application forms (page 45)

1. employment   2. surname (we can also say *family name*)   3. first name (we can also say *forename* or *given name*)   4. address   5. postcode (called *ZIP code* in American English)   6. contact   7. home   (job application forms may also ask for the applicant's *mobile* phone number and *fax* number)   8. email (also written *e-mail*)   9. education / training   10. training / education   11. attended   12. university / college   13. college / university   14. examinations / qualifications   15. qualifications / examinations   16. Degree (BA = *Bachelor of Arts*, a first university degree in Britain)   17. Diploma (RSA = the *Royal Society of Arts*, an examining body in Britain which usually provides professional / vocational qualifications)   18. history   19. present (we can also say *current*)   20. dates (we can also say *period*)   21. title   22. duties   23. reason(s)   24. leaving (note that a real job application form would also ask applicants for details of their *previous* employer(s) - the company they worked for *before* their present company)   25. referees   26. assessment   27. suitability   28. employer (compare *employer* with *employee*: an *employee* works for an *employer*)   29. approach   30. offer   31. illness   32. absence   33. absent   34. information   35. false (we can also say *untrue*)   36. dismissal (from the verb *to dismiss*)

The recruitment process (pages 46 + 47)

Part 1:
1. vacancy   2. internally (an *internal appointment*)   3. externally   4. appointments / situations vacant (informally called the *jobs pages* or *jobs section*)   5. situations vacant / appointments   6. journals   7. recruitment agency   8. institutional agency   9. job centres   10. private recruitment agency   11. description   12. applicants (from the verb *to apply*)   13. qualifications   14. experience   15. personal qualities   16. rewards (sometimes called *remuneration*)   17. increments   18. benefits   19. leave (or *holiday*)   20. discrimination   21. equal opportunities   22. affirmative recruitment   23. disabilities

Note: In Britain, the *Equal Opportunities Commission* (EOC) is the government body set up to make sure that no sex discrimination exists in employment. The *Commission for Racial Equality* (CRE) is the statutory body set up to *monitor* racial matters in companies, and to issue *guidelines* on *best practice*. Official *legislation* ensures that nobody is discriminated against (for example, the *Sex Discrimination Act* of 1975, the *Race Relations Act* of 1976, and the *Disability Discrimination Act* of 1995). Companies have a *vicarious liability* to ensure that discrimination is not a feature of the workplace.

Part 2:
1. CV (= *curriculum vitae*)   2. covering   3. introduction   4. application   5. pre-selection   6. turn down   7. short-list   8. candidates   9. one-to-one   10. board   11. psychometric   12. aptitude (compare this with an *ability test*, which only tests the candidates current skills and knowledge)   13. group-situational   14. in-basket   15. medical (sometimes just called a *medical*)

A test should have *face validity* - it should be relevant, useful and give accurate results that indicate how well the employee will perform.

continued on next page

© Bloomsbury Publishing Plc. For reference see *Dictionary of Human Resources and Personnel Management* (ISBN 0 7475 6623 2)

The recruitment process (pages 46 + 47) *continued*

<u>Part 3:</u>
1. seven-point plan   2. potential   3. appearance   4. intelligence   5. skills   6. interests   7. disposition   8. circumstances
9. references   10. offered   11. induction programme   12. temporary   13. probationary   14. open-ended / fixed-term   15. fixed-term / open-ended   16. follow-up

Personal qualities (page 48)

1. popular   2. decisive (verb = *to decide*)   3. rapport   4. punctual   5. willing   6. reliable (verb = *to rely on*)   7. critical (verb = *to criticise*)   8. sensitive   9. sensitive (note the differences in meaning of *sensitive* in these two sentences. The opposite of *sensitive* in sentence 9 is *insensitive*)   10. practical   11. judgement (spelt *judgment* in American English)   12. reserved (this is similar in meaning to *shy*)   13. impulsive   14. obstinate (we can also say *stubborn*)   15. selfish   16. sociable   17. industrious (this is <u>not</u> the same as *industrial*)   18. professional   19. conceited   20. ambition (adjective = *ambitious*)   21. motivation (verb = *to motivate*. A good worker is *self-motivated*)   22. relationship   23. confidence (adjective = *confident*)   24. abrasive   25. confrontational (verb = *to confront*)

Other qualities are also considered during interviews and appraisals. These may include *neatness of appearance, general attitude* and *approaches* to the job, *knowledge* of the organisation and / or field of work, knowledge of colleagues' work (the adjective is *knowledgeable*), the ability to communicate clearly, effectively and appropriately (verbally and on paper), the ability to *follow instructions*, the *ability to inform* managers and colleagues of problems and / or progress, *body language* and general *intelligence*.

Contract of employment (page 49)

1. Term = Terms, conditionals = conditions   2. employ = employer   3. employed = employee   4. titel = title   5. descriptive = description, duty = duties   6. locally = location   7. Celery = Salary, anum = annum, rears = arrears   8. Started = Starting (or *Start*)   9. labour = work, until = to (*Monday <u>through</u> Friday* in American English)   10. Undertime = Overtime, rat = rate   11. enticement = entitlement, anum = annum   12. Absent = Absence (or *Absenteeism* from work)   13. sceme = scheme (x2)   14. Dissiplinary = Disciplinary, grieving = grievance, handybook = handbook, police = policies   15. Probbation = Probation (x2), subjective = subject, employees = employment, note = notice   16. Terminator = Termination, probbation = probation (or *probationary*), note = notice   17. Referrals = References (x2) (a person who writes a reference is called a *referee*), apointments = appointments   18. singed = signed

Contracts of employment can be *temporary, permanent, short term, long term, fixed-term* or *open-ended*.
Contracts contain *express* terms (those that both the employer and the employee agree on), and *implied terms* (these are *not* stated in the contract, but impose obligations on both the employer and the employee).
Some contracts may contain a *restrictive covenant* (a clause which prevents an employee from doing something. For example, it may prevent the employee working for another similar company when s/he finishes work in his / her current company).
Contractual liability is a legal responsibility for something as stated in a contract.

Working hours (pages 50 + 51)

<u>Across:</u> 1. punctual (the opposite is *unpunctual* or *late*)   5. clock off (we also say *clock out*. When we arrive for work we *clock on* or *clock in*)   8. double   9. transfer   12. Regulations   13. time-keeping   15. allowed   17. half   18. graveyard   19. differentials   21. roster   24. entitlement   25. overtime   26. fixed   27. rotating
<u>Down:</u> 2. twilight   3. job-share   4. homeworking   6. full   7. part   10. flexileader   11. unsocial   14. core   16. flexilagger   20. flexitime   22. sheet   23. rotation

Note: The four main types of shift work are: 1. double day   2. day and night alternating   3. permanent night   4. 3-shift (continuous or discontinuous)

In Britain, the *Working Time Directive* of 1998 (based on guidelines set by the European Union) sets out the following regulations: Employees should work no more than 48 hours a week, and should receive a minimum of 4 weeks' paid leave a year. They should have a weekly rest period of at least 24 consecutive hours, a daily break of at least 20 minutes for every six hours worked, and a daily rest period of 11 consecutive hours. There are different directives for some groups (e.g., pilots, bus drivers, doctors, etc) whose jobs are more stressful, demand greater concentration, or whose performance might affect other people.

Appraisals (page 52)

The questions in this exercise are typical questions that might be asked at an appraisal / assessment interview (sometimes informally called *job chats*).

1. standards   2. knowledge   3. quality   4. objectives   5. improvement   6. strengths / weaknesses   7. training   8. schedule
9. progression   10. challenging   11. encouragement   12. least   13. workload   14. description   15. defined   16. advancement
17. improving   18. morale   19. relationships   20. discipline   21. treatment   22. promptly   23. complaints   24. progress
25. praise   26. facilities   27. provisions   28. benefits   29. recommend   30. comments

Normally before an appraisal, employees fill in a *self-appraisal* form. Note that appraisals / assessments are normally *knowledge-based* (what the employee knows), and *performance-based* (how well the employee has worked, and the results s/he has achieved).
Appraisals can be *two-way*, with the employee telling the company how s/he feels about it, and his / her role in it. A good company will always listen to the *feedback* it receives from its employees.
Performance-based appraisals often use a method known as *BARS* (*behaviourally-anchored rating scales*), where performance is based on a typical performance criteria set for each individual employee.   *continued on next page*

Appraisals (page 52) *continued*

Many companies have adopted the practice of *360-degree appraisals*. Colleagues above, below and at the same rank as the employee being appraised are asked to contribute their views on that employee before the interview takes place.
If an employee is not performing well in his / her current position, s/he might be given a *remedial transfer*. This means that s/he is transferred to a more suitable job. The informal expression is a *turkey trot*.

Note that many of the questions in this exercise might also be asked at an *exit interview*, when an employee is interviewed before s/he leaves the company. The questions would normally be expressed in the past tense, e.g., *Did you think...?*, *Were you happy...?*, etc. In addition to the questions in the exercise, exit interviews might also ask the employee how s/he felt about the *rewards*, *benefits* and *services* offered by the company (holiday pay, sick pay, pension scheme, health insurance, life assurance, loan facilities, educational assistance, sports and social facilities, refreshment facilities, HR services, etc).

Rewards and benefits 1 (pages 53 + 54)

Exercise 1
1. danger   2. dock   3. overtime   4. double   5. deduction   6. gross / net (*net pay* is often called *take-home pay*)   7. increment
8. minimum   9. salary   10. index   11. raise (we can also say *increase* or *hike*)   12. pension (also called a *superannuation scheme* or *plan*)   13. sub (also called an *advance* - employees can ask for an *advance on their wages / salary*)   14. bonus   15. payslip
16. payroll   17. deposit   18. package (also called a *rewards package*. This is not the same as a *pay packet*, which is an envelope containing an employee's wages)   19. arrears   20. weighting   21. income (the opposite of income is *expenditure*. Compare this with *expenses*, which is the money paid to someone to cover the costs of doing something in particular, e.g., paying for a hotel on a business trip).

Exercise 2
1. dock   2. gross / deductions   3. package   4. bonus   5. double   6. payslip   7. deposit   8. payroll   9. increment / index
10. arrears / sub

Rewards and benefits 2 (pages 55 + 56)

Exercise 1
1. direct / extrinsic   2. extrinsic / direct   3. basic   4. performance-related   5. commissions   6. recognition   7. Gainsharing
8. motivation   9. production bonus   10. premium bonus   11. attendance bonus   12. acceptance bonus (informally called a *golden hello*)   13. Profit sharing   14. benefits   15. extras   16. pensions   17. share   18. insurance   19. duvet days   20. fixed
21. flexible (also known as a *cafeteria-style benefits plan*)   22. Incentive   23. indirect / intrinsic   24. intrinsic / indirect   25. status
26. satisfaction   27. growth / development   28. skill   29. development   30. security   31. comradeship

Exercise 2
1. direct or extrinsic   2. indirect or intrinsic   3. performance-related   4. false - it is extra money paid for increased productivity
5. attendance bonus   6. extras   7. (d)   8. true   9. (c)   10. (a)

Here are some other words and expressions that you might find useful:
salaried (the adjective of *salary*)   earnings   real earnings   take-home pay   well-paid   low-paid   pay packet
pension contributions   occupational / company pension (scheme)   portable pension (scheme)   accrual rate   remuneration
hourly / daily rate   per day / per diem   a year / per annum   wage / salary review   increments   on-target earnings   parity
to erode wage differentials   incentive   basic / flat rate   broadbanding   compensation package   benefit in kind   reward
management   reward review   exploding bonus   holiday pay   sick pay   health insurance   life assurance   perks

Holidays and other time off work (pages 57 + 58)

1. medical (also called a doctor's certificate)   2. statutory (SSP = *statutory sick pay*)   3. maternity   4. unpaid   5. gardening
6. sabbatical (this word is especially used for teachers, university professors, etc, who take time away from their school or college)
7. absenteeism   8. public holiday (called a *bank holiday* in the UK, and a *legal holiday* in the USA)   9. long-service   10. entitlement
11. unauthorised (also spelt *unauthorized*. An employee who takes unauthorised leave *is* or *goes AWOL: absent without leave*)
12. waiting   13. absence   14. in lieu (usually abbreviated to *TOIL*)   15. paternity   16. casual   17. vacation   18. benefit

Letters (pages 59 + 60)

Note that the sentences for each letter are in the same order as they would appear in real letters.

1. B   2. D   3. E   4. B   5. C   6. D   7. A   8. C   9. B   10. F   11. B   12. C   13. D (this could also be used in E)   14. D   15. E
16. A   17. F   18. G   19. E   20. G   21. C   22. E   23. A   24. A   25. B   26. -   27. D   28. G   29. E   30. F   31. F   32. A
33. G   34. G   35. C   36. F

Usage notes:
* Letters that begin with a name (e.g., *Dear Mr Brown*, *Dear Ms Smith*) end with *Yours sincerely*. Letters that begin with *Dear Sir / Madam* end with *Yours faithfully*.
* Ordinal numbers (for dates, e.g., the *first* of November, the *seventh* of April) are sometimes followed by letters (e.g., *1st November*, *7th April*), but this is less common now than it used to be. *1 November*, *7 April*, etc, is more common.
* You should avoid using abbreviated dates (e.g., *12/11/05*) in formal and semi-formal letters.
* Note that modern formal /semi-formal letters should be as brief as possible. (KISS: **K**eep **i**t **s**hort and **s**imple)

You will find complete sample letters in the supplement of the Bloomsbury *Dictionary of Human Resources and Personnel Management*.

Industrial relations (pages 61 + 62)

1. e (verb = *to unionise*) 2. c 3. d 4. a 5. b 6. a 7. a (*free collective bargaining* = negotiations between management and trade unions about wage increases, etc) 8. b (compare this with a *go-slow*, where workers slow down production as a protest against the management) 9. c 10. e (workers will *down tools* and *stage a walkout*. This can also be a verb: *to walk out*) 11. d 12. c (when an arbitrator is appointed by the government, s/he is called an *official mediator*) 13. d (*strike* can also be a verb: *to strike*. A worker who strikes is called a *striker*) 14. e (when a strike is approved by a trade union, it is called an *official dispute*) 15. b 16. d (a *flying* picket is a picket who travels around the country to try to stop workers going to work) 17. d (also called a *strikebreaker*. *Scab* can also be used, although this is an offensive word) 18. c

When unions and management cannot *settle a dispute*, we say that negotiations have *reached deadlock*.

Health, safety and welfare (pages 63 + 64)

A.
1. offence 2. precautions (or *measures*) 3. officer (or *inspector*) 4. audit 5. committee 6. irregularities 7. regulations 8. representative 9. legislation 10. feature

B.
emergency exit emergency access (on a door which must be kept clear in case somebody needs to get into the building in an emergency) fire alarm fire blanket fire bucket fire door (on a door which must be kept closed at all times to stop a fire spreading through a building) fire escape fire extinguisher fire hose first aid kit fire officer first aid officer first aid post assembly point (an area outside a building where people must go when there is a fire or other emergency in a building) smoke detector

C.
1. d (*stress management* is a way of coping with stress-related problems at work) 2. c 3. a 4. b 5. b 6. d 7. b 8. a 9. b 10. c

Other words and expressions that you might find useful include:
accident book accident frequency rate accident prevention accident report criminal liability employer's liability hazard hazardous substances health and safety policy hygiene occupational disease industrial accident positive health programmes protective clothing protective equipment public health inspector / environmental health officer
Health and Safety at Work Act 1974 (HASAWA)

Discipline and problems at work (pages 65 + 66)

A.
1. timekeeping 2. absenteeism (from the adjective *absent*) 3. misconduct (this is a general word which refers to any illegal act carried out by an employee. *Gross misconduct* is very bad behaviour which is fair reason for dismissal) 4. negligence 5. breach of safety 6. sleeping 7. disobedience (from the verb *to disobey*) 8. fraud (when you use money that does not belong to you for a purpose which it is not supposed to be used, this is called *fraudulent conversion* or *conversion of funds*) 9. theft (we can use the verb to *embezzle* when an employee steals money from his / her company. The noun is *embezzlement*) 10. smoking / drinking (of alcohol) 11. dealing / using 12. bullying 13. intimidation 14. violence (*bullying, intimidation* and *violence* can also be called *aggressive behaviour*) 15. racial abuse (we can also say *racial harassment* or *racism*) 16. sexual harassment 17. damage

B.
1. dock (money that is removed as a result of misconduct is sometimes called a *financial penalty*. We can also use the verb *to fine*) 2. grievance (a *legitimate* grievance is a grievance based on a *violation* of a contract of employment) 3. hostile work environment 4. ultimatum 5. verbal warnings (a warning in the form of a letter is called a *written warning*. Employees usually receive two verbal warnings and one written warning before further action is taken) 6. sackable offence 7. letter of dismissal 8. appeal / unfair dismissal 9. insubordination 10. allegation (from the verb *to allege*) 11. aggrieved / down tools / walk-out 12. sexual discrimination 13. suspend 14. grievance procedure 15. job dissatisfaction 16. disciplinary board / disciplinary action (if an employee is unhappy with the decision made by a disciplinary board, s/he can *appeal against the decision*. Most companies have an *appeals procedure* to deal with this. *Discipline* can be a noun or a verb) 17. alienation (alienation, intimidation, poor working conditions, etc, can have an *adverse impact* on productivity) 18. instant dismissal (*dismissal* is from the verb to dismiss. *Discharge, sack* and *fire* are synonyms of *dismiss*.)

Personnel training and development (pages 67 + 68)

1. continuous personal development (also called *continual* personal development, or abbreviated to *CPD*) 2. assertiveness training 3. experiential learning (also called *learning by doing*) 4. adventure training 5. in-tray learning 6. team-building (an employee who works well as part of a team is called a *team player*) 7. carousel learning 8. sales training 9. modern apprenticeship 10. an induction course 11. off-the-job training (training which takes place on the company premises during work time is called *on-the-job training* or *in-house / in-company training*) 12. open learning 13. training needs analysis (sometimes abbreviated to *TNA*) 14. total quality management 15. online learning (also called *e-learning*) 16. action learning

Note: a trainer is somebody who trains staff, a trainee is somebody who learns how to do something.

Here are some other words and expressions that you might find useful:
adult education correspondence course distance learning training needs performance appraisal staff appraisal team learning individual learning autonomous learning learning curve learning style evaluation and assessment work-based learning INSET (in-service training) Investor in People (a national programme for employee development sponsored by the UK government) managerial grid